En

MW00986494

"This is a good introduction to baptism, written in an irenic spirit and covering a wide range of relevant material. I expect that many will find this helpful and will come to a richer appreciation of what baptism signifies."

—Dr. Robert Lethem
Professor of systematic and historical theology
Union School of Theology, Oxford, England

"Dr. Richard is a sure and trusted guide on the issue of baptism. This is a delightful resource, particularly for paedobaptists. It will be a go-to and concise guide to give to parents who are bringing their covenant children for baptism. An absolutely essential resource."

—Dr. Derek W.H. Thomas
Senior minister
First Presbyterian Church, Columbia, S.C.

BAPTISM

BAPTISM

ANSWERS TO COMMON QUESTIONS

GUY M. RICHARD

Reformation Trust   A DIVISION OF LIGONIER MINISTRIES, ORLANDO, FL

Baptism: Answers to Common Questions
© 2019 by Guy M. Richard

Published by Reformation Trust Publishing
A division of Ligonier Ministries
421 Ligonier Court, Sanford, FL 32771
Ligonier.org   ReformationTrust.com

Printed in Ann Arbor, Michigan
Cushing-Malloy, Inc.
0001218
First edition

978-1-64289-024-2 (Paperback)
978-1-64289-025-9 (ePub)
978-1-64289-026-6 (Kindle)

Cover design: Ligonier Creative
Interior design and typeset: Katherine Lloyd, The DESK

Unless otherwise noted, Scripture quotations are from the ESV® Bible (The Holy Bible, English Standard Version®), copyright © 2001 by Crossway, a publishing ministry of Good News Publishers. Used by permission. All rights reserved.

Scripture quotations marked NASB are taken from the New American Standard Bible® (NASB), Copyright © 1960, 1962, 1963, 1968, 1971, 1972, 1973, 1975, 1977, 1995 by The Lockman Foundation. Used by permission. www.Lockman.org

Library of Congress Cataloging-in-Publication Data

Names: Richard, Guy M., author.
Title: Baptism : answers to common questions / Guy M. Richard.
Description: Orlando, FL : Reformation Trust Publishing, a division of
   Ligonier Ministries, [2018] | Includes bibliographical references and index.
Identifiers: LCCN 2018025629 (print) | LCCN 2018038612 (ebook) | ISBN
9781642890259 (ePub) | ISBN 9781642890266 (Kindle) | ISBN 9781642890242
Subjects: LCSH: Baptism--Presbyterian Church--Miscellanea.
Classification: LCC BX9189.B3 (ebook) | LCC BX9189.B3 R53 2018 (print) |
   DDC 234/.161--dc23
LC record available at https://lccn.loc.gov/2018025629

To Schyler, Jane Barton, and Ellie

May you each cherish your baptism
and strive continually to improve it
for the rest of your life

CONTENTS

Introduction. 1

1. What Is Baptism? 9

2. Does Baptism Mean Immersion? 15

3. What Does Baptism Mean? 23

4. Why Do We Baptize, and How Should We Do It? 31

5. Who Should Be Baptized? 41

6. What Do the "Household" Baptisms Teach Us? 53

7. Why Do Our Baptist Brothers and Sisters Disagree? 65

8. How Do We Respond to the Baptist Arguments? 71

9. But What about Jeremiah 31? 81

10. What Objections Do We Have to Baptizing
    Believers Only? 91

11. What Can We Take Away from All This?. 101

    Notes 117

    Scripture Index 123

    About the Author 129

INTRODUCTION

As a Presbyterian pastor, I get asked questions about baptism more often than about any other issue in the church except, perhaps, predestination. The questions I receive range from the basic—What is baptism?—to the much more complex—Why do you baptize your children? Sometimes the people asking the questions come from a tradition that practices believers-only baptism. They have never had to think through what they believe on this topic because they have never actually encountered a plausible challenge to what they have been taught. Sometimes the questioners are newcomers to the Reformed faith and have not steeped in its teachings long enough to see the strength of the biblical argument for infant baptism. Sometimes they come from within the Presbyterian tradition, but they have never stopped to consider why or how we administer baptism or to compare and contrast our views with the views of our Baptist brothers and sisters.

What makes the questions so difficult is that, more often than not, people are asking them on the way out of church on Sunday morning. I have found it nearly impossible in these situations to offer answers that are concise enough to fit into the time constraints imposed by the receiving line and yet are clear enough to cause the questioners to think more about the topic and to challenge their preconceived ideas.

Good answers to these questions require more than a one- or two-minute explanation. They are not easily or explicitly answered by a quick Bible reference. Even a topic as difficult as predestination might be easier to explain than baptism. (Note that I said easier to *explain*, not easier to *accept!*) In answering questions about predestination, I can simply point people to Romans 9, for instance, and tell them to go home and read it and then come back and discuss it with me. But I cannot assign one or two passages of Scripture to answer questions about baptism. Explaining baptism requires a more extended examination of many different Bible texts that must be pulled together (or systematized) in order to develop a picture of what the Bible as a whole teaches on the issue. *Theological*

Another complicating factor is that oftentimes it is not the explicit teaching of various passages but their obvious implications that help us develop a clearer picture of what the Bible teaches about baptism. This, too, makes it more difficult to give a short answer to people's questions. Seeing and understanding these implications requires more sustained thought and interaction than we are able to do on the way out of church on Sunday morning. And it means that we need a more extended format—like this book, for instance—to walk people through the whole of the Bible's teaching. *a book is needed?*

But it also means that we need to be prepared for a built-in suspicion that many people—especially those within the evangelical Protestant tradition—have toward things that appear overly complicated. As Mark Noll has argued in his insightful and challenging book *The Scandal of the Evangelical Mind*, evangelical Christians have historically tended to value action over thinking and simplicity over complexity. They have not been interested in devoting the time and energy necessary to sustain complex thought and argumentation because they have instead been "dominated by the urgencies of the moment."[1] Canadian scholar N.K. Clifford puts it this way: "The Evangelical Protestant mind has never relished complexity. Indeed its crusading genius, whether in religion or politics, has always tended toward an over-simplification of issues and the substitution of inspiration and zeal for critical analysis and serious reflection."[2]

As evangelical Christians, we tend to think that simpler is better, and we lose patience with long and complex argumentation. We are suspicious about any doctrine that requires complicated arguments to support it. Surely, we think, God does not intend for us to go to great lengths and to unravel great complexities in formulating or defending our doctrine, does He? *Good thought, maybe accurate*

In responding to this suspicion, we need to point out first that many of the most important theological doctrines of the Christian faith cannot be defended with one or two proof texts but require an extended and oftentimes complicated examination of Scripture. The doctrines of the Trinity, the union of the two natures of Christ in one person, and the nature and extent of the atonement are good examples of this. Each requires a detailed and somewhat complicated examination of the whole of the Scriptures. Baptism is no different, and this leads us to our second point.

We need to remember that *everyone's* answers to the common questions about baptism are going to be somewhat complicated—or, at least, they should be. That is because the Bible is not explicitly clear on its answers to many of these questions. Take the question about the proper recipients of baptism. There is no verse in the Bible that says, "Thou shalt baptize your children." There is also no verse in the Bible that says, "Thou shalt *not* baptize your children," or, "Thou shalt baptize only adult believers." The same thing can be said about the mode of baptism. There is no verse in the Bible that says, "Thou shalt baptize by immersion," and there is no verse that says, "Thou shalt baptize by sprinkling."

[handwritten margin note: argument from silence]

[handwritten margin note: evidence]

The fact that the Bible is not explicit on these questions does not mean that we should refrain from attempting to answer them. We need to search the Scriptures and to do our best, using all the tools at our disposal, to understand what the Bible teaches regarding the proper recipients of baptism. The lack of explicit teaching in the Bible simply means that we have to work a little harder and dig a little deeper to find the answers to our questions. And that is true for everyone who takes up this issue.

[handwritten note: → But the Bible doesn't answer everything]

In the third place, we must respond to the built-in suspicion toward complicated argumentation by reminding people that Jesus instructed us to study the Bible by way of drawing out the relevant implications of every text of Scripture—no matter how small or complicated those implications may be—and formulating our theology accordingly. We can see an example of this in Matthew 22:29–32, where Jesus chastises the Sadducees for denying the doctrine of the resurrection. He tells them that their denial demonstrates that they know "neither the Scriptures nor the power of God" (v. 29). Thus, in Jesus' opinion, the Sadducees should have known about the doctrine of the resurrection because it is implied in Exodus 3:6: "I am the God of Abraham, and the God of Isaac, and the God of Jacob" (Matt. 22:32). Based only on the tense of the verb—I *am*, not I *was*—Jesus says that the Sadducees should have deduced that God is not the "God of the dead, but of the living," and, therefore, they should have embraced the doctrine of the resurrection instead of rejecting it. In other words, Jesus says, the Sadducees had a responsibility to study not only the explicit teaching of every passage of Scripture but also its implicit teaching and to build their theology accordingly, no matter how tedious or complex the arguments may have become. And you and I have this same responsibility.

It is with all of this in mind that I am writing this book. I hope to provide answers to many common questions about baptism and to do so in a more thoroughgoing way than I am able to do in casual conversations or on Sunday mornings at church. Many of my answers will necessarily be more complicated than they would be if I could simply cite a Bible verse or two. And many of my answers will be based on the clear implications of passages that do not explicitly deal with the topic of baptism. But, thanks both to accepted theological practice in regard to other doctrines and to Matthew 22:29–32, I know that I stand on safe theological and exegetical ground in doing these things.

My goal in writing this book is to get readers to think through what the Bible teaches about baptism—whatever conclusions they may come to. Far too often as evangelical Christians, we pass over the hard task of searching the Scriptures and thinking through what is actually said in favor of accepting someone else's conclusions or embracing what seems to make sense to us without ever critically evaluating the biblical text. I hope to challenge Christians to engage with Scripture on this topic and to come to their own conclusions as to what the Bible teaches. That engagement is itself an indispensable part of how we are to "be transformed by the renewal of [our] mind[s]" (Rom. 12:2).

In my own context as a pastor, I have actually had quite a few seasoned Christians admit to me over the years that they had never really thought about the issue of baptism before coming to our church. They had always assumed that the obvious examples of baptism in the New Testament were clear and strong enough evidence to warrant applying it only to believers after they had made a profession of faith. This admission is one of the main reasons that I started devoting an entire class period of the new members class to the topic of baptism. I want to get people thinking about what the Bible actually teaches about baptism—regardless of whether they are convinced by my arguments.

But my goal in putting this book together is also to challenge Christians who may disagree with one another on this topic to deal with each other more graciously than they have in the past. The topic of baptism as a whole—<u>but especially the topic of the proper recipients of baptism</u>—has been far too divisive within the church for far too long. It is important for all of us to realize and to acknowledge that, regardless of where we come down on this question, we are all wrestling with what the Bible actually teaches. It is not that one side in the baptism debate is appealing to explicit passages of Scripture to support its views while the other is appealing only to its implications. Both sides are appealing to the <u>implicit</u> teaching of Scripture, because, as we have indicated, the Bible is not explicit on many of the common questions that we have about baptism. And it is not that one side in this debate is appealing to Scripture to support its views while the other is appealing to tradition or history. Both sides are appealing <u>primarily to Scripture</u> and are coming to different conclusions on what the Bible teaches. If people in the church could only acknowledge these things and treat each other accordingly, we would all be a lot better off.

We need to remember that the debate surrounding baptism is a family debate. Those who disagree with me on this topic are my brothers and sisters through faith in Jesus Christ. We are family—members of the one "household of God" (1 Tim. 3:15). Moreover, we are all members of the one body of Christ. We are united to Christ and, thereby, united to one another. To borrow the imagery of the human body that Paul uses so effectively in 1 Corinthians 12:12–26, some of us are hands, some are feet, some are fingers, and some are toes, but all of us are part of the same body. For us to fight over issues like

Can both be right?

baptism is like fingers fighting with hands or toes fighting with feet or one hand fighting with the other hand. By all means, we need to discuss these matters, and we may even disagree. That is OK. Disagreement is not a bad thing, in and of itself. Disagreement can be helpful. It can bring clarity and focus. But the *way* we disagree and what we do with that disagreement are important. We need to remember these things and keep them in mind as we tackle this topic. We are on the same side, and we are engaged in the same endeavor, namely, to discern the will of God in all things and to be as faithful to Him as we can be. It is in that spirit that I offer the following discussion on the topic of baptism.

Before moving on, it bears mentioning that there is a great deal of agreement between Christians on the topic of baptism. For instance, we all agree that Christian baptism is important; that it should involve the application of water to the individual; that it should be done in the name of the Father, the Son, and the Holy Spirit (see Matt. 28:19); and that it is linked inextricably with faith (either on the part of the person being baptized or on the part of at least one parent of the one being baptized). The areas of disagreement—though they have taken center stage—are not the whole story. There are many areas of agreement between Christians in regard to baptism, and it is important to point that out at the beginning of our examination.

CHAPTER 1

WHAT
IS BAPTISM?

If we were to start reading the New Testament from the beginning, we would not be able to get very far before we encountered something called baptism. As early as Matthew 3:1, we run into a man by the name of John, who is otherwise known as "the baptizer," and, a few verses later, we see why. This John, we are told, devotes his life to "baptizing" many different people (vv. 6, 7, 11), the Lord Jesus Himself being one of them (vv. 13–17). The baptisms that we encounter in these early chapters of Matthew's gospel are described simply as occurring. Very little explanation is given as to how they were performed or why they were performed. We are left to conclude that the practice of "baptism," whatever it is, must have been something that was familiar to Matthew's Jewish audience in the first century.

The same thing can be said for all the baptisms that we see in the New Testament. Thus, when Jesus commands His followers to go and make disciples in Matthew 28:18–20, He instructs them to baptize those disciples in the name of the Father, Son, and Holy Spirit. But He nowhere explains what He means by baptism, and we nowhere read that the disciples were confused by what He was saying. None of the remaining eleven who were with Him raises his hand or interjects with a question. They all appear to understand what Jesus is talking about.

When we turn to the Old Testament, we find evidence that the Jews had some kind of familiarity with the concept of baptism. The same Greek words that occur in the Gospels are used in the Septuagint—the Greek translation of the Hebrew Old Testament—on several occasions. And since the Septuagint predates the birth of Christ by a good bit, we know that first-century Jews would have had some idea of what baptism was long before John the Baptist came onto the scene.[1]

The account of Naaman in 2 Kings 5 is one occasion in the Old Testament that is particularly instructive in terms of helping us understand the Jewish mind-set toward baptism. Naaman was the commander of the army of the king of Syria, a man of tremendous courage and might, but he had leprosy (v. 1). Through a series of providences, Naaman was directed to go and seek healing from the prophet Elisha. When he arrived at the prophet's house, he was commanded to "wash in the Jordan [River] seven times" in order to be clean (v. 10). But we read in verse 14 that Naaman went and *baptized* "himself seven times in the Jordan, according to the word of the man of God, and his flesh was restored."[2] The significant thing about this passage is the fact that "wash" in verse 10 and "baptize" in verse 14 are

10

used interchangeably. Naaman was commanded by Elisha to "wash" in order to be healed, and he "baptized" himself and was restored to health.

Hebrews 9:10 is another significant passage that helps shed some light on the Jewish understanding of baptism leading up to the first century. It tells us unequivocally that the Old Testament ceremonial system, long before the time of Christ, included many different kinds of ritual "baptisms."[3] Although this passage does not explicitly tell us which specific kinds of rituals were known as baptisms, it does alert us as to their presence in the Old Testament. Because the context of Hebrews 9 is talking about the temporary rites and practices of the ceremonial system, it is not a great stretch to see the ritual washings of the regulations for clean and unclean people as being chiefly in mind here. When we look back at these ritual washings (of which there are at least eleven), we see the repeated requirement to wash garments, objects, and people in water in order to rid them of their ceremonial uncleanness. Sometimes this washing is partial, as in Exodus 30:18–21, in which the priests are commanded to wash only their hands and feet before entering the tabernacle. Sometimes it is wholesale, as in Leviticus 14, where individuals are commanded to wash their whole bodies and also their clothes. In all these cases, however, washing or cleansing in water is the common feature.[4]

Thus, when we consider the example of Naaman from 2 Kings 5 together with the many ritual baptisms from the Old Testament, we are able to conclude that the first-century Jew would have regarded baptism as a rite of washing or cleansing in

1st century Jew – washing or cleansing in water

= cleansing or purification

water. The way this water would have been applied would have
been less important than the meaning behind its application.
For the first-century Jew, baptism would have meant cleansing
or purification, and it would have been applied directly to the
person who is unclean in the sight of God in order to wash him
and render him clean or pure before God.

A New Testament Rite

What about Jesus' baptism?

In the New Testament, after the death of John the Baptist,
we see baptism taking on added significance. It becomes the
outward sign of the new covenant people of God. We see this
particularly in Matthew 28:18–20, where Jesus commands His
followers to make disciples of all nations and peoples and to
mark them out with water baptism. We also see it in Acts 2,
when Peter instructs would-be followers of Christ to "repent
and be baptized" (v. 38). The point is that, beginning with the
end of Christ's earthly ministry, all who turn to Jesus in faith
are to be marked out with the sign of baptism. It is something
that everyone who puts his faith in Christ must now do. These
two passages, among others, coupled with the clear statements
in the New Testament indicating that circumcision no longer applies to new covenant Christians (see, for example, Acts
15 and Gal. 2:3–10; 5:7–12; 6:12–16), lead us to conclude
that baptism takes on added significance in the ministry of
the Apostles and the early church. It is still an outward rite of
washing or cleansing with water, just as it was in the Old Testament, but it is now specifically commanded by the Lord to

Infants can't have faith

be administered to every disciple as an outward sign of God's covenant with them. → *assumes to those of physical descent*

If we allow that baptism functions in the same way in the New Testament that circumcision did in the Old—a point that I will be arguing in a later chapter—then Romans 4:11 is an important passage in formulating an answer to our question, What is baptism? This passage states that circumcision functioned as a "sign . . . and seal of the righteousness that [Abraham] had by faith."[5] Circumcision was a sign that represented or pointed to the right standing that Abraham had in the sight of God, a standing that he had received by faith. It was an outward reminder that Abraham had been changed, an external marking that indicated he belonged to the Lord and was in covenant with Him. Circumcision did not earn Abraham his acceptance with God. It simply marked him out as one who was in right standing with God already. It was a visible pointer to an inward spiritual reality that belonged to Abraham by faith. *Agree*

But, according to Paul, circumcision was not just a sign; it was also a seal or an official imprint or inscription. The word that is used here is reflective of a signet ring that would be pressed into hot wax to certify the official character of a document or of a high-ranking official's seal that would guarantee the authenticity of some correspondence from or action by that official. The point is that circumcision was designed to function as a guarantee to Abraham confirming all the promises of the covenant to him. It marked him off as belonging to the Lord in a visible way and confirmed to him his rightful place in the covenant.

13

Conclusion

If in fact baptism does replace circumcision in the New Testament, then this means that baptism functions in the same way that circumcision did, namely, as a sign and seal of the righteousness that is ours by faith. It is an outward sign that points to an inward spiritual reality and marks us out as belonging to the Lord. It is a confirmation that everything Jesus accomplished on the cross is ours by faith in Him.

With this in mind, we can say that baptism is a rite of washing or cleansing in water that is commanded by the Lord Jesus Himself to be a sign and seal of the inward washing of all our sins and thus of being counted righteous in God's sight only through faith in Jesus Christ.

CHAPTER 2

DOES BAPTISM MEAN IMMERSION?

Some of our fellow brothers and sisters in Christ maintain that the word *baptism* actually means immersion. But this assertion does not hold up under close scrutiny. In order to substantiate their claims, our brothers and sisters must prove that the word *baptism* always and only means immersion. It is not enough to show that it sometimes means immersion or even that it usually means immersion. But a quick survey of the New Testament is enough to show that the word *baptism* does not always and only mean immersion. In fact, there are several times when the word must mean something else.

Perhaps the clearest and most significant example of this is found in Acts 2, the account of the day of Pentecost. We know that this event is in fact a "baptism." Jesus Himself specifically refers to it as such in Acts 1:5 (see also Matt. 3:11 and parallels). We might even say that it is *the* baptism; it is the inward reality to which water baptism points. In Acts 1:8, Jesus describes this baptism as the Holy Spirit "coming upon" His disciples. In Acts 2:3, the Spirit is said to have "rested on" them. And on three separate occasions in Acts 2, we are told that the mode of Spirit baptism is not immersion but *pouring* (see vv. 17, 18, and 33). The most important baptism in the New Testament is thus not described as an immersion at all but as an affusion, or a pouring out, of the Holy Spirit upon the disciples. Incidentally, this is the primary reason why Presbyterians, Episcopalians, Anglicans, and Methodists—just to name a few—administer baptism by sprinkling or pouring. *The* baptism of the New Testament was clearly administered in this way. Its example is enough to show that the word *baptism* ought not be restricted to meaning immersion.[1]

But there are other passages in the Bible in which the word *baptism* cannot be taken to mean immersion; see, for example, Leviticus 14:6, 16, 51; 1 Corinthians 10:2; and Hebrews 9:10. Of these passages, the first and the last are particularly significant. Hebrews 9:10 tells us that there were "various baptisms" or washings that were a part of the purification rites of the Old Testament ceremonial system. Some of these ceremonial baptisms appear to have been immersions, but not all of them. Some of them clearly involve sprinkling or pouring, and some do not indicate how they were administered at all.

Leviticus 14:6, 16, 51 describes portions of the purification rite for cleansing a person with leprosy. In verses 6 and 51, we read that the priest was to take two birds, kill one of them, and then "dip" the other in the blood of the one that was killed. In verse 16, we are told that the priest was to "dip" his right finger in oil that was in the palm of his other hand. In each of these cases, the word "dip" is translated by the word *baptō* in the Septuagint. Linguistically, *baptō* is very closely related to the more common New Testament words for baptism, *baptizō* and *baptisma*. This is significant because, in all of these cases in Leviticus 14, the particular way in which the rite takes place cannot be immersion. One bird simply would not supply enough blood for another of the same kind to be fully immersed. And the palm of the hand cannot contain enough oil for immersion to take place. The point of the passage is not immersion. The point is not even about a particular mode of the rite. The point is about the meaning of what is being done in this rite, namely purification.

These passages support the contention that the word *baptism* cannot always and only mean immersion. It might sometimes mean that, or even many times. But the word must have a larger and more comprehensive meaning.

The Emphasis Is Not on Mode

When we look at the examples of actual water baptism that we see in the New Testament, we really do not see any particular mode advocated. These baptisms could have been administered by immersion or by pouring. We are not told. *argued from silence*

To be sure, some people have taken the prepositional phrases used in connection with these baptisms as evidence for immersion. But this is saying too much. When the text states that "they went down into the water" or that "they came up out of the water," it is possible that it indicates immersion as the mode. But we cannot say this for sure. These phrases actually reveal nothing about the mode of baptism. Anyone who walks down the bank of a river to stand in that river is said to "go down into the water" and to "come up out of the water" when they walk up the bank. The same point can be made more clearly perhaps when we consider sand traps on a golf course. When a golfer hits his ball into the trap, he will "go down into" the bunker to get it and hit it and then "come up out of" it afterward. But we do not mean to imply that this golfer was immersed in the sand when we say that he "went down into it" or "came up out of it." The same is true of these examples of baptism. It is quite possible that two people went down into the river to stand there in water, and one reached down and took some water and poured it on the one being baptized. The prepositional phrases do not answer this question for us. ~~Poor argument~~

There is an interesting example in the book of Acts that would seem to support the idea that the prepositions "down into" and "up out of" cannot be used to refer to mode. It is found in Acts 8, the account of Philip and the Ethiopian eunuch. In verse 38, we read that Philip and the eunuch "both went down into the water." If this prepositional phrase is indicative of immersion, then, in this case, *both* Philip and the eunuch were immersed, because we are told that *both* went down into the water. But the very next verse says that Philip baptized the eunuch, indicating that, if immersion is meant, the eunuch alone would have "gone down into the water." Since the text says that both went down into the water, the prepositions cannot refer to any particular mode of baptism. Otherwise, both Philip and the eunuch would have been baptized. The prepositions are simply describing the action of walking down into the water from a position of being outside the water. Both did that. But only one was baptized. And we do not know how he was baptized, because the text does not tell us.

The ceremonial "baptisms" in the Old Testament (see Heb. 9:10) are often a great deal more explicit about the particular mode that should be applied. Some are clearly called sprinklings, and some are called full-body washings. But even in these more explicit situations, the mode seems to be treated as less important than the meaning of what is being done. In Numbers 19, for instance, the modes of "sprinkling" and pouring (vv. 13, 18–20) and "washing" and "bathing" (vv. 19, 21) are all used together as part of the cleansing ritual for an unclean person. This would seem to suggest that the important thing was the cleansing itself, not the particular way in which it came to pass. We see the same thing in Leviticus 14, where "sprinkling" (v. 7) and "washing" (v. 8) are used together in the cleansing of lepers. The important thing is not that any one mode of administering the washing is being applied but the fact that the unclean person is being washed.

We should, therefore, be wary of assigning too much weight to any one mode of administering baptism. The New Testament examples of water baptism do not seem to indicate how each baptism was performed, and the Old Testament examples place their importance on the meaning of what is being done rather than on any one particular way of doing it. All of these things demonstrate that the word *baptism* does not always mean immersion. And if it does not always mean immersion, then it cannot be defined in those terms. We must look for a better definition to take into account the variations in meaning that we see.

A Common Objection Addressed

One important implication of showing that *baptism* cannot be defined as immersion is that it allows us to address a common objection to the practice of applying baptism to the children of believers. The objection goes something like this: since the word *baptism* means immersion, and since no one in their right mind would ever immerse an infant, this means that baptism must be applied to adults only. But, since *baptism* cannot be taken to mean immersion, the whole tenor of this objection is overturned.

It must be said, however, that even if the word *baptism* is taken to mean immersion, it is not at all clear that this would determine the proper recipients of baptism. There is no scriptural, medical, or legal prohibition against infant immersion. Why should we think that immersion would somehow eliminate infants as recipients? Greek Orthodox churches and some Brethren congregations continue to practice infant immersion successfully today. The mode does not necessarily determine the recipients. We should not forget that God commanded Abraham to circumcise his own infant sons without any of the advantages of our modern medical technology. Why would immersing them momentarily be any more gruesome or risky?

CHAPTER 3

WHAT DOES
BAPTISM MEAN?

If baptism does not mean immersion, then what does it mean? There are at least four main things that are signified in Christian baptism. They are (1) washing or cleansing from sin, (2) Spirit baptism, (3) union with Christ, and (4) union with other believers. All four are envisioned in the Bible's teaching about the meaning of baptism. We will look at each in turn and then examine which of the four seems to be the primary meaning.

Washing or Cleansing from Sin

Frequently in the Bible, Christian salvation is described in terms of washing or cleansing. Perhaps the most well-known example of this is found in Psalm 51, which contains David's heartfelt prayer of repentance after his public failure with Bathsheba. On at least three different occasions in this psalm, David pleads with the Lord that he would be cleansed of his sins and washed "whiter than snow" (vv. 2, 7, 10). Several passages in the New Testament also speak of Christian salvation as a washing away of all our sins (see 1 Cor. 6:9–11; Eph. 5:25–26; Titus 3:5). And several others adopt the language of cleansing from sin and defilement to distinguish what it means to be a Christian (see 2 Cor. 7:1; Heb. 10:2; 1 John 1:7–9).

Since salvation is frequently described in terms of washing, and since baptism involves the application of water to the body, it is not difficult to conclude that there must be a link between the outward washing of baptism and the inward washing of the forgiveness of our sins. But when the verses mentioned above are combined with the "various baptisms" of the Old Testament that we have addressed previously—all of which were rites of purification designed to cleanse the individual from ceremonial defilement—this link becomes even clearer. The Old Testament background to the New Testament practice of baptism thus prepares us to see the strong connection that must exist between baptism and washing or cleansing from sin. As water applied to the body cleanses the outward person of all physical dirt and defilement, so the blood of Jesus cleanses the inward soul of the spiritual dirt and defilement of sin. The two go hand in hand.

Spirit Baptism

As we have already seen, Jesus refers to the pouring out of the Holy Spirit at Pentecost as a baptism in Acts 1:5. This in and of itself links receiving the Holy Spirit with water baptism. But the connection becomes stronger when we see that receiving the Holy Spirit is really of the essence of Christian salvation. Paul says that quite plainly in Romans 8:9: "Anyone who does not have the Spirit of Christ does not belong to him." Paul's point here is that the fundamental difference between the non-Christian—who is described as being "in the flesh" in verse 8—and the Christian—described as being "in the Spirit"—is that the Christian has the Holy Spirit living within him. If someone does not have the Holy Spirit, then he cannot really be a Christian.

Paul calls the Holy Spirit the "Spirit of Christ" because the Spirit's work is to take Christ and all that He accomplished on our behalf and to apply it to the believer. It is Jesus Christ who lives within the Christian in and through His Holy Spirit. Thus, the Spirit is called the Spirit of Christ. As Paul says elsewhere, the Christian's "hope of glory" is none other than "Christ in you" (Col. 1:27).

With this in mind, we can understand everything that is involved in being a Christian as contained in the idea of being baptized in the Holy Spirit. When we receive the Spirit, we receive Christ and all His benefits. When we receive the Spirit, we are washed of all our sins and cleansed from all our unrighteousness. This means that water baptism and Spirit baptism are connected not only because they are both baptisms, but because water baptism actually points to Spirit baptism.

Moreover, the connection between Spirit baptism and water baptism provides the warrant for our applying the latter

Water baptism highlights Spirit baptism

in the same way that the former is applied. Since Spirit baptism is applied by way of a sprinkling or pouring out upon the individual, this suggests that water baptism ought to be applied in the same way. Those who disagree with me on this point do so because of what we will talk about next.

Union with Christ

The close relationship between Spirit baptism and water baptism ensures that there will also be a close relationship between water baptism and union with Christ. When the Holy Spirit, the Spirit of Christ, takes up residence in the believer, He unites that believer to Jesus Christ. Paul says as much in Romans 6:3–5:

> Do you not know that all of us who have been baptized into Christ Jesus were baptized into his death? We were buried therefore with him by baptism into death, in order that, just as Christ was raised from the dead by the glory of the Father, we too might walk in newness of life. For if we have been united with him in a death like his, we shall certainly be united with him in a resurrection like his.

Here Paul describes Spirit baptism in terms of being buried with Christ in His death and being raised again with Him to new life. This is one reason why many Christians choose to apply water baptism by way of immersion. They believe that it depicts this action of being buried with Christ in His death and being

26

raised again with Him to new life. There certainly is something appealing about that symbolism. Union with Christ is clearly central to what water baptism is intended to portray. What is not so clear is whether immersion alone can portray it or whether sprinkling can also do it. We will revisit that question shortly in our discussion of which meaning of baptism is primary.

Union with Other Believers

Because the Holy Spirit unites all believers to Christ, He necessarily unites them to one another as well. Thus, Paul says that when we receive the baptism of the Holy Spirit, we are "all baptized into one body—Jews or Greeks, slaves or free" (1 Cor. 12:13). We all become part of the one body of Christ. We are connected to Him as fingers, hands, arms, legs, and toes are all connected to the human body. And because we are connected to Him, we are connected to one another. "The eye cannot say to the hand, 'I have no need of you,' nor again the head to the feet, 'I have no need of you,'" because every part of the body is connected to every other part (v. 21). Water baptism signifies this connection as well. We are "baptized" into this connection.

Which Meaning Is Primary?

Some Christian brothers and sisters have suggested that among all these meanings for baptism, the one that should be considered primary is union with Christ. The eminent professor John Murray of Westminster Theological Seminary was one such Christian brother.[1] He believed that the language used to describe baptism in the New Testament reflects an emphasis on union with Christ. Thus, we are said to be "baptized into" the Father, the Son, and the Holy Spirit (Matt. 28:19) or Christ (Rom. 6:3) or Moses (1 Cor. 10:2) or Paul (1 Cor. 1:13). Murray also believed that passages such as Romans 6:3–6, 1 Corinthians 12:13, and Colossians 2:11–12 teach that baptism ought to represent visibly the believer's union with Christ in His death, burial, and resurrection, and that this ought to be the "basic and central import" of what baptism is all about.[2]

While there is no doubt that union with Christ is a vital part of what is intended to be portrayed in Christian baptism, it is not clear that this ought to be considered its primary meaning. I say this for two main reasons, the first of which is grounded in the Old Testament background to Christian baptism. We know from Hebrews 9:10 that the Old Testament ceremonial system included "various baptisms" and that these were all cleansings or washings designed to teach the Israelites their need to be washed of their defilement before God. In each of these cases, as we have already argued, the meaning of cleansing is of primary importance, far more than any one way of achieving that cleansing.

In the second place, the fact that water is the requisite element that is to be used in baptism suggests that cleansing or washing should be considered the primary meaning of the rite. If union with Christ was intended to be primary, any number of other ways of demonstrating this could have been employed. Being buried in the ground, for instance, and then raised up out of the ground would have pointed to union with Christ more effectively than water. Even simply lying down on the ground and then being raised up from a prone position would have been better than water, especially since the word *baptism* cannot be taken to mean immersion and since the New Testament appears to be agnostic on the question of the mode by which baptism should be applied.[3] Because water is required, because we are not commanded to apply that water in any particular way, and because the Old Testament background to baptism points to washing, cleansing or washing must be considered the primary meaning intended in Christian baptism.

What does water symbolize in the OT
- flood → death
- Red Sea → death
- Jordan River → passing into the promised land
-

CHAPTER 4

WHY DO WE BAPTIZE, AND HOW SHOULD WE DO IT?

Simply stated, the reason why we baptize is because God commanded us to do so. In such passages as Matthew 28:18–20 and Acts 2:38, we are instructed by Jesus or His Apostles to baptize everyone who repents and puts his faith in Christ. That in and of itself is good enough reason to do it.

Other passages highlight the importance of baptism for Christians. One such passage is 1 Peter 3:21, which states, "Baptism . . . now saves you." Peter is not teaching that water baptism can actually procure salvation for us. This would contradict the more clear teaching of Scripture that we see in other places, such as Ephesians 2:8–9. Our salvation is not tied to any work that we do or any action that we take. It is tied wholly to the work that Christ has already done, which we simply receive through faith. So Peter cannot be teaching that baptism actually saves us. But he does seem to be identifying the sign of baptism with what it signifies, namely, salvation—which does speak to the importance of baptism.

God Himself does something similar in Genesis 17:10, where He says to Abraham, "This is my covenant, which you shall keep, between me and you and your offspring after you: Every male among you shall be circumcised." Here God identifies the sign of the covenant, circumcision, with what it signified, namely, the covenant itself—so much so that He speaks of them both interchangeably. The covenant is spoken of as the sign, and the sign is spoken of as the covenant. The two go hand in hand. That seems to apply equally to Peter's words in 1 Peter 3:21. He speaks of salvation in terms of baptism because of the close relationship that exists between the two of them. The two go hand in hand.

This means that it is wrong for us to ignore or delay baptism. The sign and the thing signified are intended to go together. When we follow a public profession of faith in Christ with water baptism, we protect the integrity of the sign and the thing signified. But we also protect it when we apply it to the children of at least one believing parent. The sign and the thing signified are still linked. The sign is linked with the parent's faith and with the faith that the parent hopes and prays will soon come to fruition in the child. I think that is what Peter has in mind when he says that baptism is thus "an appeal to God for a good conscience, through the resurrection of Jesus Christ" (1 Peter 3:21).

→ Parents on behalf of their children?

Baptism Is Not Necessary for Salvation

Given what we have just said, it must also be pointed out that baptism is not necessary for salvation. Being baptized will not guarantee someone entrance to heaven, and not being baptized will not condemn him to hell. We know that from the example of the thief on the cross in Luke 23:39–43. This thief, after witnessing Jesus going through the ordeal of the cross with grace and after hearing His words, repented and believed in Christ in the waning moments before he died on his own cross. He believed, but he was never baptized. There was no opportunity. And yet Jesus still pronounced that the thief would surely be with Him that very day in "paradise" (v. 43), which obviously indicates that it is not necessary for anyone to be baptized in order to be saved.

It ought to be a tremendous comfort for those who may be near death and yet have never been baptized to know that this oversight will not keep them out of heaven. While baptism is clearly important, it is not necessary in order to be saved. This also ought to be a tremendous comfort for those who believe that they were baptized in an illegitimate way or that their baptism somehow did not "take" the first (or even the second) time. Well-meaning Christians can sometimes give the impression that baptism must be applied in a certain way at a certain time to be valid. And, as a result, Christians can often struggle with doubt over whether their baptism was valid. The fact that baptism is not necessary to be saved ought to be a source of tremendous encouragement for all such people.

Baptism Is an Outward Application of Water

As we have indicated, the Bible is silent on the particular mode by which water baptism ought to be applied. Therefore, we should not be dogmatic when it comes to mode. We should go as far as the Bible goes and no further. For this reason, it seems best to conclude that the mode by which baptism is applied is immaterial.

The mode of Spirit baptism in Acts 2—which is unequivocally a pouring out on the individual—seems to indicate that sprinkling or pouring is a valid mode for the application of water baptism. Likewise, the fact that the word *baptism* can mean immersion at times and the fact that some of the Old Testament ritual baptisms were immersions indicates that immersion is also a valid mode for water baptism. The important thing is not the mode that the baptism takes but the meaning behind it, which is cleansing or washing with water. *I think it means Union of X.*

This means that the use of water is a nonnegotiable element of Christian baptism. We are not free to use juice or blood or any other liquid—not that we would want to, anyway—if the goal is to celebrate Christian baptism. Water has an integral part in the administration of this rite. In Acts 8:36, in the account of Philip and the Ethiopian eunuch, we read that the eunuch, upon encountering water as they traveled, asked to be baptized: "See, here is water! What prevents me from being baptized?" He recognized that the presence of water was at least one necessary precondition for his baptism.

How Many Times Should We Be Baptized?

One practical question about baptism deals with the number of times that baptism ought to be administered to the same person. I recently had a conversation with a member of my previous congregation who was struggling with doubt over whether any of his baptisms were valid. He had already been baptized three times—as an infant, as a child after making a public profession of faith for the first time, and again as a young adult after his church had convinced him that neither of the previous two baptisms had been valid. As a result of all these baptisms and the teaching that he received about why he needed them, he was wrestling with serious doubt about whether he had ever been truly baptized. At the same time, he was also struggling with regret over allowing himself to be baptized so many times.

I have seen other Christians struggle similarly because they feel the need to be rebaptized after making a profession of faith, either because they do not remember their original baptism or because they want to do something to make a public demonstration of their newfound faith. In all of these cases, however, there is one and the same root problem: a misunderstanding about what baptism is really all about.

Baptism is a sign, and by definition, a sign is meant to point to what it signifies or represents. The location of the sign is less important than the presence of it. When I get onto Interstate 85 in Atlanta and drive north toward Greenville, S.C., I do not need many signs along the way telling me that I am on the right

Bap. is a sign

road. I only need one sign telling me that I am on I-85 North. I know that as long as I stay on the interstate (even if I get off occasionally for a short time), I will arrive in Greenville in due course. I don't need another sign after I arrive in Greenville to tell me that I have arrived. I know that I have arrived, because the original sign pointed me in the right direction. The same is true with Christian baptism. It is a sign that points us in the right direction, toward the washing away of our sins. As long as we stay on the road (even if we do get off course occasionally), we do not need another sign to know that we have reached our destination.

This means that we should not look to be rebaptized. Once we have received the sign that points us in the right direction, we do not need to receive it again.

Interestingly, when we look at Scripture, we do not see any clear examples of rebaptism anywhere. This is perhaps most telling in the account of Simon the Magician in Acts 8:9–24. In this account, we are told that Simon responds to the preaching of Philip by believing in Jesus and being baptized (vv. 12–13). But after Simon sees the Holy Spirit being given to the people by the Apostles, he offers them money to be able to do what they have just done. Peter responds to Simon by saying: "May your silver perish with you, because you thought you could obtain the gift of God with money! You have neither part nor lot in this matter, for your heart is not right before God. Repent, therefore, of this wickedness of yours, and pray to the Lord that, if possible, the intent of your heart may be forgiven you. For I see that you are in the gall of bitterness and in the bond of iniquity" (vv. 20–23).

Based on this interaction between Peter and Simon, we can infer that Simon's original profession of faith (in v. 13) was not in fact genuine. Not only does Peter indicate that Simon will "perish" with the silver he has offered (v. 20), but he goes so far as to say that Simon's "heart is not right before God" (v. 21). Simon was apparently baptized after a false profession of faith. With that in mind, it is utterly fascinating that Peter does not say to Simon, "Repent and be baptized." That is what he clearly said after Pentecost to the great crowd of people in Jerusalem who had neither repented nor been baptized. But here in Samaria, Peter only says, "Repent." He apparently does not need to tell Simon to be baptized again, because Simon was already baptized once. The fact that his baptism took place after what appears to be a false profession of faith made no difference.

Some brothers and sisters have claimed that Acts 19:1–7 offers a clear example of rebaptism. In this passage, the Apostle Paul meets some "disciples" (v. 1) in Ephesus who had only been baptized "into John's baptism" but had apparently never heard of Jesus or the Holy Spirit. After Paul tells them about Jesus, we read in verse 5 that "they were baptized" for, what would appear to be, a second time "in the name of the Lord Jesus." But it is not so obvious that this passage is actually commending rebaptism. In the verses immediately preceding this passage, in Acts 18:24–28, Apollos is described in terms that are similar to those applied to the "disciples" of chapter 19; he is said to have known "only the baptism of John" (18:25). But we read nothing of his being rebaptized, even though Priscilla and Aquila had to pull him aside—as Paul did with the "disciples" in chapter 19—and explain "to him the way of God more accurately" (v. 26). Why, then, would John's baptism suffice in one context but not in the other? Could it be that something more is going on in chapter 19?

It is possible that chapter 19 is not actually referring to water baptism at all. This is John Calvin's take on the matter.[1] And the biblical text certainly seems to bear his understanding out. Thus, in verse 2, we are told that the very first thing Paul asks these "disciples" is whether they received the Holy Spirit when they believed. Paul's question sets the stage for the remainder of the passage and suggests that the baptism that Paul has in mind is not water baptism but the baptism of the Holy Spirit. If we read verse 5 in this light, it appears that Paul is in fact talking about Spirit baptism and not about being rebaptized with water. Verse 6 also lends support to this reading by offering the details as to how the baptism of the Holy Spirit came to pass. The two verses (vv. 5–6) then form a unit, according to well-known conventions of Hebrew storytelling in which a general overview of the events is provided first and the specific details are given afterward.[2] This is the same storytelling method that Moses uses so effectively in Genesis 1 and 2 to narrate the events of creation.

When we read Acts 19 in conjunction with the account of Apollos in Acts 18 and the account of Simon the Magician in

Acts 8, we see further evidence supporting the idea that water baptism is probably not in mind in chapter 19. Apollos was not rebaptized in Acts 18; neither was Simon in Acts 8. Why would we think the "disciples" in Acts 19 would be? It seems best to conclude that they were not.

CHAPTER 5

WHO SHOULD BE
BAPTIZED?

[handwritten margin notes: professed faith before bp? / 4 out of 12 - professed full bpt / 8 out of 12]

It is obvious from the New Testament that those who profess to believe in Jesus Christ for the first time, having never been baptized previously, are to receive the outward sign of water baptism. In at least eight of the twelve instances of Christian baptism in the New Testament, we see the same basic series of events unfolding: one or more people profess to believe in Jesus and then receive the outward sign of that faith.[1] This idea is in keeping with the Old Testament practice of circumcision, which was applied to Abraham as an adult after he had believed (Rom. 4:9–11). As a result, we can look for the practice to continue beyond the Apostolic period into our own day. So, in accord with what we see in Old and New Testaments, we know that all those who are old enough to profess faith in Christ for themselves, and actually do so, should be baptized. But are there any others who should be baptized as well? What about the children of believers?

Should Our Children Be Baptized?

Many well-intentioned people begin to answer this question by citing the three "household" baptisms found in Acts 16 and 1 Corinthians 1, or Jesus' attitude toward the little children in the Gospels, as their proof that baptism should also be applied to the children of believers. The appeal to "household" baptisms is not as helpful as it might seem at first. It is possible that children were a part of one or more of the "households" that were baptized, but we are not told that in these texts. We need to be very careful not to read into the text things that we might want to be there. It is also possible that these "households" included only adults. But, again, we need to be very careful here. The texts do not say anything about what these households looked like. They simply state that the entire households were baptized.

Jesus' attitude toward little children is more helpful in this discussion, and more will be said about this attitude at a later point. But there is still a better place to begin answering the question of whether our children should be baptized. We need to begin with the Old Testament. If we look at the household baptisms and the passages about Jesus and the children apart from the Old Testament Jewish context that serves as the foundation for the whole of the New Testament, we will never see the real strength of the argument for infant baptism. Thus, to answer the question best, we need to begin in the Old Testament. We need to understand the Old Testament context out of which the New Testament came.[2] Then, and only then, can we turn to the New Testament and examine the household baptisms and Jesus' attitude toward little children and other such passages. Only then will we see those passages in their proper light.

So, we will begin by looking at Genesis 17, specifically verses 11–13. In these verses, God is speaking to Abraham and to the descendants who would come after him, and He tells them: "You shall be circumcised in the flesh of your foreskins, and it shall be a sign of the covenant between me and you. He who is eight days old among you shall be circumcised. Every male throughout your generations, whether born in your house or bought with your money from any foreigner who is not of your offspring, both he who is born in your house and he who is bought with your money, shall surely be circumcised."

Here we read quite plainly that God commanded the outward sign of His covenant with Abraham and his descendants—that is, circumcision—to be applied to infants and children, even from eight days old. What is not so plain, however, is how this applies to us today. As we think this through, three questions come to mind: (1) What is the relationship between God's covenant with Abraham and God's new covenant with us today? (2) What is the relationship between circumcision and the Abrahamic covenant? and, (3) What is the relationship between circumcision and baptism? Once we answer these questions, we will be better equipped to understand the basic argument for applying baptism to our children in the church.

What Is the Relationship between
Genesis 17 and the New Covenant?

The covenant that God entered into with Abraham in Genesis 17 (see also Gen. 12; 15) was not an earthly, temporal covenant promising earthly, temporal (and geographical) blessings. It was not a national covenant enacted with the physical and geographical nation of Israel. It was a spiritual covenant promising spiritual blessings. It was a covenant that was, at its heart, very much like the new covenant that God has entered into with you and me today. To be sure, there were national aspects of the Abrahamic covenant. But these national aspects were intended by God for a spiritual fulfillment and purpose.

We see this in several key passages of Scripture, such as Hebrews 11:8–10: "By faith Abraham obeyed when he was called to go out to a place that he was to receive as an inheritance. And he went out, not knowing where he was going. By faith he went to live in the land of promise, as in a foreign land, living in tents with Isaac and Jacob, heirs with him of the same promise. For he was looking forward to the city that has foundations, whose designer and builder is God." From this we see that God's covenant definitely had an earthly and geographical dimension to it. Land was clearly promised to Abraham and to his descendants in verses 8 and 9. But verse 10 tells us that this earthly dimension of God's promise was not the end that God had in mind—it was only a means to the end. The physical land and earthly inheritance were only intended to point Abraham and his descendants forward to a permanent land and a permanent inheritance that God had "built" and "designed" for them to enjoy, which was heaven itself. This, and not an earthly promised land, was the ultimate end of God's covenant with Abraham and his descendants.

The same thing can be seen a few verses later in Hebrews 11:15–16. This time, it is much more obvious that the author is speaking of heaven, because he mentions it by name: "If they [Abraham and Sarah] had been thinking of that land from which they had gone out, they would have had opportunity to return. But as it is, they desire a better country, that is, a heavenly one. Therefore God is not ashamed to be called their God, for he has prepared for them a city." The point in these verses is that Abraham and Sarah were not ultimately looking ahead to an earthly "better country" but to a heavenly one. The earthly promised land was only intended to point Abraham and his descendants to the heavenly promised land that was to come. That was what was really being held out to them in the covenant that God had entered into with them. ⇒ OC

We also see the spiritual nature of the Abrahamic covenant in Romans 4, where the Apostle Paul specifically connects Abraham to new covenant Christians by citing Abraham as an example of one who was "saved" in the same way that we are as Christians, that is, through faith alone. Abraham's faith looked ahead to Jesus (see John 8:56) and to heaven. Our faith looks back to the same Jesus and ahead to the same heaven. That is why Paul says that "it is those of faith who are the sons of Abraham" (Gal. 3:7). It was that way in the Old Testament, and it is still that way today. The Abrahamic covenant was never intended to be a purely national covenant enacted with Abraham and his natural or biological offspring. It was always intended to be a spiritual covenant enacted with Abraham and his spiritual offspring.

We see this even more clearly in Galatians 3, where Paul plainly tells us that the Abrahamic covenant was made with Abraham and his *offspring*—not "offsprings." It was made with his one offspring, Jesus Christ (v. 16). Thus, all who believe and are "in Christ" are the real sons of Abraham, regardless of whether they are biologically descended from him. The Abrahamic covenant and the new covenant are connected. One flows out of the other. Jesus, *the* offspring of Abraham, ensures this. That is why Paul can say in Romans 4 that Abraham is the father of those who are uncircumcised (i.e., gentiles) but who believe as he did and are justified as he was *and also* the father of those who are circumcised (i.e., Jews, his biological descendants who would be circumcised at eight days old) and then later genuinely put their faith in Christ as Abraham himself did (vv. 11–12). And it is also why Paul can refer to the "blessing of Abraham" not in terms of land or physical offspring but in terms of the Holy Spirit (Gal. 3:14).

What Is the Relationship between Circumcision and the Abrahamic Covenant?

Some Christian brothers and sisters are fond of saying that circumcision was only intended to be an external way of distinguishing the nation of Israel from every other nation. It was a badge of identification, they argue, much like a driver's license or passport is today. It marked off the members of the nation of Israel and distinguished them from all others.[3]

But there are at least a couple of problems with this assertion. First, there was no nation of Israel in existence when God commanded Abraham to circumcise himself and his descendants. It was not until Jacob and his twelve sons (Abraham's grandson and great-grandsons) that the nation of Israel began to take shape. Most of Abraham's descendants would eventually constitute the nation of Israel, but not all of them. Ishmael, Abraham's son through Hagar, is one notable exception. He had no part in the nation of Israel. But he was clearly circumcised (see Gen. 17:25). The same thing could be said of the foreigners whom God explicitly commands Abraham to circumcise in Genesis 17. They were not Israelites. But they were connected to Abraham as members of his household and were subject to his headship, and so they were to be circumcised.

The second problem in claiming that circumcision is merely a badge of national identity is that the Bible repeatedly states that circumcision was intended to be an outward sign pointing the people to their need for an inward "circumcision of the heart." In Deuteronomy 10:16, for example, we read that God commanded Israel to circumcise "the foreskin of your heart, and be no longer stubborn." In context, this is a clear call to repentance, which is necessary before Israel would ever be able to meet God's requirements "to fear the LORD your God, to walk in all his ways, to love him, to serve the LORD your God with all your heart and with all your soul, and to keep the commandments and statutes of the Lord" (vv. 12–13).[4]

Deuteronomy 30:6 takes this a step further and expressly links the inward circumcision of the heart to loving God and thereby obtaining life: "And the Lord your God will circumcise your heart and the heart of your offspring, *so that you will love the Lord your God with all your heart and with all your soul, that you may live*" (emphasis added). Before Israel could love the Lord with all their heart and soul, and thus live, their hearts first needed to be circumcised. They needed the uncleanness and rebellion of their hearts cut away.[5] They needed their inward resistance to God and their stubborn refusal to keep His commands to be removed.[6] Physical circumcision was not sufficient. They needed to be circumcised on the inside with a spiritual circumcision "made without hands," to borrow Paul's language in Colossians 2:11.

We see this again in Jeremiah 9:25–26, when God promises that He will bring judgment on all those who are uncircumcised in heart and flesh (gentiles), as well as on all those who are circumcised in their flesh but not in their heart (biological descendants of Abraham who do not inwardly and genuinely love and serve God).[7] The point is obvious. God was not interested in outward circumcision per se. He was interested in inward circumcision of the heart. He was interested in outward circumcision only insofar as it was a visible reminder of or a pointer to what needed to take place on the inside. It was a physical sign pointing to a spiritual and inward reality; it was not an ethnic badge of identification.

it was a badge 48
of ID + ...

When we turn to the New Testament, we see this same idea confirmed in the book of Romans. In chapter 4, Paul states unequivocally that circumcision was a sign and a seal of "the righteousness that [Abraham] had by faith" (v. 11). It, therefore, cannot be regarded as a physical and external mark of Israel's ethnicity; it must be seen as a physical and external mark that pointed to a spiritual and inward reality. Abraham was "justified," that is, declared to be right with God, by his faith. And the outward sign and seal that was given to Abraham to remind him and to assure him of his standing before God was circumcision. It was not a badge of national identity. It was a spiritual sign pointing to a spiritual and inward reality—in Old Testament language, to a circumcision of the heart. ⟹ *made through faith in X.*

The Abrahamic covenant was never ultimately about physical descendants and physical promises and blessings. It was always about spiritual descendants and spiritual promises and blessings. It was never ultimately about physical circumcision. It was always about spiritual circumcision of the heart. Outward circumcision was intended to be a pointer either to what had already happened on the inside—in the case of adults such as Abraham who were circumcised on the inside first and then on the outside—or to what they hoped and prayed and anticipated would happen on the inside—in the case of infants who were circumcised on the outside at eight days old. Sometimes those who received outward circumcision as infants were never circumcised on the inside. Ishmael and Esau seem to be good examples of that.[8] But the point is, the Abrahamic covenant was never about the physical; it was always about the spiritual. It was never about the external; it was always about the internal.

What Is the Relationship between Circumcision and Baptism?

In order to answer this question, we need to look more closely at Colossians 2:11–12. Here Paul takes up the spiritual and inward aspects of circumcision and connects them with the spiritual and inward aspects of Christian baptism: "In [Christ] also you were circumcised with a circumcision made without hands, by putting off the body of the flesh, by the circumcision of Christ, having been buried with him in baptism, in which you were also raised with him through faith in the powerful working of God, who raised him from the dead."

In these verses, Paul is speaking of spiritual circumcision and spiritual baptism and applying them both to the Christian. After everything we have been saying about the Abrahamic covenant, we would expect Paul to apply the image of spiritual circumcision to the New Testament Christian. As Galatians 3:29 states, all who belong to Christ are "Abraham's offspring, heirs according to promise." Christians are the real descendants of Abraham. They have been circumcised on the inside. We would expect Paul to say that, and he does. But he also says more. He goes on to speak of spiritual baptism and applies that image to the Christian as well. Both spiritual circumcision and spiritual baptism apply to the New Testament

Christian. Both capture the essence of what it means to be a believer.

That tells us at least two important things. First, it tells us again that New Testament Christians are in continuity with the Abrahamic covenant. That is why Paul can yet again speak of believers in Abrahamic terms. Physical circumcision is no longer important (see Acts 15:1–21, among other places in the New Testament). But what physical circumcision was intended to represent and point to—an inward circumcision of the heart—is still every bit as important for us today.

Second, Paul's statement in Colossians 2 also signals the fact that physical baptism has now replaced physical circumcision in the life of the New Testament Christian. We see this in at least two ways. One, we see it in connection with the explicit passages stating that circumcision is no longer required (e.g., Acts 15:1–21) but that baptism is required for the New Testament Christian (e.g., Matt. 28:19; Acts 2:38). Two, we see it in Colossians 2, where Paul applies what physical circumcision represents (spiritual circumcision of the heart) *and* what physical baptism represents (spiritual baptism by the Holy Spirit, who unites us to Christ) to the individual believer. These two factors mean that the Christian will be the one who has been circumcised spiritually and inwardly *and* baptized spiritually and inwardly *but only* necessarily baptized physically and outwardly (i.e., not necessarily circumcised, because circumcision is no longer required in the new covenant). The point is that Colossians 2 suggests that baptism functions in the same basic way that circumcision did in the Old Testament.

(handwritten margin notes: "disagree ?", "× Fulfilled it.", "?", "Both circumcised & baptized spiritually ⇒ Baptized phy. & outwardly")

Conclusion

Thus, we see that the Abrahamic covenant is essentially the same as the new covenant because it is made with Christ, and all who are in Christ are, therefore, children of Abraham and members of the covenant God enacted with him. Moreover, we also see that circumcision functioned under the Abrahamic covenant in the same basic way that baptism functions in the new covenant—both are outward signs of an inward and spiritual reality. And we see that circumcision is replaced by baptism as we move from the Old Testament into the new covenant economy. Bearing all these things in mind, we would expect that if God commanded Abraham to apply the outward sign of the covenant to his biological children, even from eight days old, then we should be doing the same thing for our biological children, unless there were specific instructions in the New Testament that we should not. → *argument from silence*

How about circumcision is fulfilled in X! insted of being replaced

CHAPTER 6

WHAT DO THE "HOUSEHOLD" BAPTISMS TEACH US?

If the line of reasoning in the previous chapter is correct (that the Abrahamic and new covenants are essentially the same), then we would expect to see evidence of it in the New Testament practice of baptism. While there is no doubt that the majority of the baptisms we see in the New Testament are adult baptisms that follow a profession of faith in Christ, there are at least three examples of "household" baptisms as well.[1] Twice in Acts 16 and once in 1 Corinthians 1, we see occasions in which an entire household was baptized without any clear indication of whether the entire household believed. Not much detail is given in 1 Corinthians 1, but the two passages in Acts 16 are worthy of further study.

The Household of Lydia Is Baptized

In Acts 16:11–15, Lydia is converted as the Lord "opened her heart to pay attention to what was said by Paul" (v. 14). We are explicitly told that she was baptized "and her household as well" (v. 15). Now, it is possible that everyone in her household believed in Christ as she did. But we are not told this, so we cannot make this assumption. All we are told is that *she* believed, and then *she and her entire household* were baptized. It is also possible that there were infants or young children in that household. But, again, we are not told this, so we cannot make this assumption either.

If we think about this from a Jewish perspective (i.e., from the perspective of the Abrahamic covenant), this is exactly what we would expect to see. We would expect that when Lydia believed, she would receive the outward sign of baptism herself, and her entire household would as well. That is Genesis 17 carried over into the New Testament, with baptism replacing circumcision. When Abraham believed, he received the outward sign of circumcision (which pointed to an inward circumcision of the heart), and his entire household received the same sign, regardless of whether they believed. They did not receive the sign based on their own faith.[2] They received the sign based on Abraham's faith. When the head of the household believed, every member of the household was to receive the outward sign of inclusion in the covenant community regardless of whether they believed for themselves. And that is precisely what we see in Acts 16. Lydia believes, and her entire household is baptized regardless of whether they believed. argument from silence

54

Remember that the New Testament was written in a Jewish context and that most of its authors were Jewish men who had received the outward sign of God's covenant when they were eight days old. The practice of "household" circumcisions was well known by these men. They had experienced it their whole lives. "Household" baptisms would have been exactly what these men expected, given that baptism had replaced circumcision as the outward sign of God's covenant.

But not only had these men experienced the household principle of God's covenant, they had learned about it as well. It was a part of their longstanding history as the people of God dating back at least to the time of the Noahic covenant, generations before Abraham even walked the face of the earth. They knew that the household principle played an integral part in God's redemptive purposes in and through Noah. They knew the same things that we know from Genesis 6:8, 18, namely, that Noah found "favor" (literally, "grace") in the sight of the Lord but that the benefits of this favor extended beyond Noah to "all [his] household" (Gen. 7:1).[3] Even though God established His covenant with Noah ("you" in v. 1 is second-person singular), all who were associated with Noah or connected to him—his wife, his sons, and his sons' wives—received the benefits of the covenant. The authors of the New Testament would have known this.

Thus, there is no reason to read into the account of Lydia's conversion. We do not need to assume that her entire household was converted. We can take the passage at face value and see that it is in perfect continuity with the household principle

BAPTISM

that we see in the Old Testament beginning at least with Noah and with the practice of household circumcision that we see instituted in Genesis 17 and then modified in the New Testament by the substitution of baptism for circumcision (Col. 2:11–12).

The Household of the Philippian Jailer Is Baptized

In Acts 16:25–34, we see a second instance of household baptism, this time in the account of the conversion of the Philippian jailer. Once again, we are told that the head of household was converted and that he and his entire household all received baptism. There is, however, a slight difference between this passage and the previous passage about Lydia. For one thing, this account seems to suggest that everyone in the jailer's household may have believed. Look, for instance, at verses 30–32: "Then [the jailer] brought [Paul and Silas] out and said, 'Sirs, what must I do to be saved?' And they said, 'Believe in the Lord Jesus, and you will be saved, you and your household.' And they spoke the word of the Lord to him and to all who were in his house."

It could be that Paul and Silas were foretelling the future when they said that the jailer and his household would all be saved. And it could be that this idea is reinforced by the fact that Paul and Silas then went on to preach the Word of God to the jailer and to his entire household. What is more, verse 34 could add support to this interpretation, at least as the verse appears in some English translations—most notably the NIV,

KJV, NASB, and NKJV. These translations all state that the jailer's household joined him not only in his rejoicing but in his believing as well.

If it is true that the jailer and his entire household were converted, then all the members of the household would have received baptism in the same way that Abraham received circumcision in Genesis 17, namely, after believing for themselves. This in no way contradicts the practice instituted with Abraham but is in complete harmony with it, which is exactly what we would expect if there were no infants or young children in the household and everyone was able to hear the Word of God and to respond in faith.

But is it true that the entire household was converted? There is at least one good reason to answer this question in the negative. In light of the Old Testament household principle evident in the Noahic covenant and of the Old Testament household practice of circumcision instituted in Genesis 17, a first-century Jewish reading of the account would likely have understood that the jailer alone was converted but that the benefits of the covenant extended beyond him to his entire household.

But even if this is not true, the very least we can say is that we cannot definitively answer the question of whether the members of his household believed. In the first place, there is a great deal of uncertainty in connection with this passage. It could be that Paul and Silas were foretelling the future when they said that the jailer and his household would be saved. But it could also be that they were simply telling the jailer what would happen if they all did believe—that is, if he and his household believed, they would all be saved.

Another possible explanation is that Paul and Silas were merely using the language of Genesis 17. Peter does that in Acts 2:38–39, when he says: "Repent and be baptized every one of you in the name of Jesus Christ for the forgiveness of your sins, and you will receive the gift of the Holy Spirit. For the promise is for you and for your children and for all who are far off, everyone whom the Lord our God calls to himself." This passage, in fact, may shed some light on the account of the Philippian jailer because of what Peter says in verse 39. Verse 38 seems to say everything necessary: "Repent and be baptized every one of you" applies to everyone, children and foreigners included. There is no need to add that the promise extends to children and foreigners. So, why mention them? It seems that Peter was holding out something special to these children and foreigners (i.e., those children and foreigners who were associated with the households of all who were hearing him and who had been "cut to the heart" and asked, "Brothers, what shall we do?"). Peter, who was a Jew, probably had the promise of Genesis 17 on his heart and mind. Just as the promise to Abraham applied not only to himself but to his children and to every foreigner who was in his household, so the same thing is true in the New Testament. Paul and Silas may also have had this promise in mind in Acts 16.

The point is that we cannot say for certain that Paul and Silas were telling the future in Acts 16:31 or if they were simply making a free offer of the gospel. It may well be that they were using the covenantal "household" language of Genesis 17, just as Peter did before them. This practice and language would have been ingrained in them as Jews from birth.[4]

In the second place, we cannot definitively answer the question about whether the jailer and his household were all converted because several English translations render Acts 16:34 as stating explicitly that the jailer was the only person who believed (among them the ESV, RSV, and NRSV). Verse 34 in the Greek is not as clear as we might like it to be. The ESV's rendering of it may well be the most accurate: "Then [the jailer] brought [Paul and Silas] up into his house and set food before them. And he rejoiced [third-person singular, referring to the jailer] along with his entire household [adverb] that he had believed [singular participle, referring to the jailer] in God."

Here, the English phrase "along with his entire household" is only one word in the original Greek, an adverb, which follows the main subject/verb "he rejoiced" and precedes the participle "he had believed." The question we have to answer is, Does the adverb in this case modify the preceding main verb or does it modify the succeeding participle? Modifying the main verb would be the most natural reading, but the other is also a distinct possibility. If the adverb modifies the main verb, then the ESV's translation is correct, and the sense of the verse is that the jailer alone believed.[5] If it modifies the participle, then the NASB's translation is correct ("having believed in God with his whole household"), and the sense of the verse is that the jailer and his entire household believed.[6] The point is that we cannot say with certainty that everyone in the household believed. The uncertainty among the English translations underscores this fact.

What we can say with certainty is that the jailer believed and that the jailer and his entire household were baptized. It may well be that the entire household believed, but we cannot say that with certainty, and the more natural reading of the verse suggests otherwise. So, if we limit ourselves to what we can say for sure, we see the exact same situation that was described in the account of Lydia and her household. This too, then, would be in complete harmony with the provisions made concerning circumcision in Genesis 17.

Jesus' Attitude toward Little Children

Outside of the household baptisms, we can also point to Jesus' attitude toward little children during His earthly ministry. In Matthew 19:13–15 (parallels in Mark 10:13–16; Luke 18:15–17), we are told that parents were bringing their "children" (Matt. 19:13) to Jesus so that He might lay His hands on them and pray for them. Apparently, these children also included some "infants" (Luke 18:15) who were small enough to be held "in his arms" (Mark 10:16). There are several significant features of this account. The first is that the parents would even think to bring their children to Jesus at all. Surely this is reflective of the high place that children had always had in God's covenant community. The promise of Genesis 17 was not only for Abraham; it was also for his children. These parents obviously believed that Jesus would receive their children favorably. That is why they brought them to Him in the first place.

The second significant feature is the anger that Jesus shows toward the disciples for trying to keep the children from coming to Him. According to Mark, Jesus was "indignant" at this (Mark 10:14) and instructed His disciples not to "hinder them" from coming to Him (v. 14; cf. Matt. 19:14; Luke 18:16). Apparently, Jesus thought that His disciples—who were all Jews, steeped in the provisions of Genesis 17—should have known better.

The third significant feature is what Jesus says and does. In response to the disciples' efforts to prevent the children from coming to Him, Jesus says, "Let the little children come to me and do not hinder them, for to such belongs the kingdom of heaven" (Matt. 19:14). This response is fascinating. According to Jesus, the reason that the disciples should allow the children to come to Him is because "to such belongs the kingdom of heaven." Surely, in light of the Old Testament context, this means more than that these children were simply examples of what adults must do to belong to God's kingdom. Surely it means that these children themselves had a rightful place in the external covenant community (we will say more about this in chapter 8). Many of these children could not *do* anything. They were infants. If Jesus is simply using these children as object lessons to teach adults that they need to have a childlike faith, then how do the infants fit into His lesson? Jesus cannot be saying that adults need to have an "infant-like" faith or an "infantile" faith. Moreover, why would Jesus bless the children if He only means them to be an object lesson to teach adult believers?

No doubt, part of what He is saying here is that adults need to have a faith that trusts God implicitly in a childlike way in order to belong to the kingdom of heaven. But the presence of infants in the story shows that He must also mean something more, namely, that these children are entitled to all the privileges of the kingdom of heaven in the same way that children had been entitled to all the privileges of the covenant community of God ever since the time of Abraham. Jesus likely was not saying that these children were necessarily "saved," any more than Esau was "saved" in the Old Testament. But I do think He was ascribing to these children the same kind of privileges and blessings that Esau would have enjoyed as a child of the covenant. Jesus' attitude toward these children is in clear harmony and complete continuity with both Genesis 17 and the household principle we see in the Noahic covenant.

When the children are finally permitted to come to Him, Jesus does something that is equally as fascinating as what He says to His disciples. Jesus lays His hands on the children and blesses them (Mark 10:16). This is one of only two occasions in the New Testament where we are told that Jesus pronounces a blessing on others. The other is in Luke 24:50–51, where Jesus blesses His disciples immediately before ascending into heaven. The fact that little children are one of only two groups of people that we see Jesus blessing in the New Testament ought to be enough in itself to make us see the passages about them in a completely different light.

But Jesus' blessing of the little children is different from the blessing He pronounces on His disciples. The blessing that Jesus gives to His disciples is performed by raising His hands and speaking to them as a collective whole. But with the children, Jesus takes each one in His arms and blesses them one by one. How could Jesus do this if He thought these children were outside of God's covenant community until and unless they professed faith in Him for themselves? What is the basis upon which He does this? The fact that Jesus blesses these little children indicates that there was a special relationship in place already that warranted His blessing them. These children—just like those under the Abrahamic covenant—were entitled to all the privileges and blessings that come with inclusion in the external covenant community.

Are we pressing this passage too far? Some of our Christian brothers and sisters would certainly think so. They point out that this story of Jesus' blessing the little children has nothing to do with infant baptism. And, of course, they are right that the word *baptism* does not occur anywhere in the passage. Jesus is not teaching about baptism, at least not explicitly. But He is displaying an attitude toward children and infants that is in keeping with the principle behind infant baptism, and that is the principle of covenant inclusion. Ever since the time of Noah in Genesis 6–7 and the time of Abraham in Genesis 17, the children of believers were seen as different. They were not like the pagan adults living in the nations all around Israel. And they were not like the pagan children of those pagan adults. They were in a kind of relationship with God. They had access to God. They had the privilege of hearing about God and listening to His Word and watching it being lived out in the lives of their parents up close and personal. They were children of the covenant. Jesus' attitude toward the little children and especially His blessing them are not only consistent with this covenantal approach but are clearly reflective of it. That has tremendous implications for our view of baptism.

Conclusion

The New Testament contains evidence that supports the application of baptism to the children of believers. When at least one head of a household believes in Christ, the entire household is entitled to receive the outward sign of God's covenant. The head of the household receives baptism as a sign pointing back to the profession of faith that he or she has already made. The household receives it as a sign pointing ahead to the profession of faith that the head of household hopes and prays will come in the future as a result of the influence and the spiritual seasoning that is introduced into that household by his or her newfound faith.

CHAPTER 7

WHY DO OUR BAPTIST BROTHERS AND SISTERS DISAGREE?

We know that our Baptist brothers and sisters disagree with us about the proper recipients of baptism. They believe that baptism is rightly administered only to those who believe in Jesus for themselves. They believe this for one or more of the following reasons: (1) they see essential discontinuity between the Abrahamic covenant and the new covenant, (2) they do not see the connection between circumcision in the Old Testament and baptism in the New Testament, (3) they see the obvious examples in the New Testament as favoring a believers-only approach to baptism, and (4) they believe the doctrine of the church requires that baptism be applied to believers only. We will briefly explain each of these considerations in the current chapter, and then, in the next chapter, we will attempt to answer each one.

Discontinuity between the Abrahamic and New Covenants

David Kingdon is an advocate of the believers-only position on baptism. His book *Children of Abraham* is arguably the best and most objective treatment of the scriptural justification for the believers-only position. In this book, he admits that there is some continuity between the Abrahamic covenant and the new covenant. But he maintains that whereas the former was made with the biological descendants of Abraham, the latter was made only with his spiritual descendants. Thus, while he acknowledges something of a link between circumcision in the Old Testament and baptism in the New, he cites a fundamental shift in the recipients of each covenant sign because he sees a corresponding shift in the membership of each covenant. In the Old Testament, the biological children of Abraham were entitled to receive the sign of the covenant (circumcision) because, he says, the Abrahamic covenant was made expressly with them. But in the New Testament, only the spiritual children of Abraham—those who believe—are entitled to receive the sign of the covenant (baptism) because the new covenant is made with them and with them alone. In both covenants, he argues, it is the children of Abraham who receive the covenant sign, but the children have changed in the new covenant from biological children to spiritual children who exercise faith in Jesus Christ.[1] ⟶ through sp. birth (John 3)

To support these claims from Scripture, Kingdon looks especially to Jeremiah 31:31–34:

Behold, the days are coming, declares the LORD, when I will make a new covenant with the house of Israel and the house of Judah, not like the covenant that I made with their fathers on the day when I took them by the hand to bring them out of the land of Egypt, my covenant that they broke, though I was their husband, declares the LORD. For this is the covenant that I will make with the house of Israel after those days, declares the LORD: I will put my law within them, and I will write it on their hearts. And I will be their God, and they shall be my people. And no longer shall each one teach his neighbor and each his brother, saying, "Know the LORD," for they shall all know me, from the least of them to the greatest, declares the LORD. For I will forgive their iniquity, and I will remember their sin no more.

Based on this passage, Kingdon argues that the new covenant will be different from (or "not like"; v. 32) all the earlier covenants that God made with Israel. It will be different in the sense that the new covenant will be composed of believers only. Every previous covenant, Kingdon claims, including the Abrahamic covenant, was made with the nation of Israel, which included some individuals who were genuinely and inwardly God's people and some who were so only externally (see Rom. 9:6–8). But now for the first time, beginning with the new covenant, believers, and only believers, will be a part of God's covenant people. Thus, we read in Jeremiah 31 that (1) all the members of the new covenant will have the law written on their hearts (v. 33), (2) they will all be God's people (v. 33), and (3) they will all know the Lord and be forgiven of their sins (v. 34).

If Kingdon is right about Jeremiah 31, then he would certainly seem to have a legitimate argument that the Abrahamic covenant is made with Abraham's biological children while the new covenant is made with his spiritual children. If Kingdon is right that the members of the new covenant are indeed different from those of the Abrahamic covenant, then the connection between circumcision and baptism fails. And if this connection fails, then Presbyterians, Episcopalians, Anglicans, and Methodists—in addition to many others—will lose the biblical basis upon which they baptize the children of professing believers. The question is, Is Kingdon right about these things?

Discontinuity between Circumcision and Baptism

Kingdon sees discontinuity not only between the Abrahamic covenant and the new covenant but also between circumcision and baptism—enough, he thinks, to undercut the position of all who hold to infant baptism. His claim is that circumcision had more of a national emphasis in the Old Testament than baptism does in the New. To highlight the difference that he sees between the Abrahamic covenant and the new covenant, he asks whether participation in the earthly and temporal aspects of the Abrahamic covenant was enough to secure a right to circumcision.[2] In other words, Kingdon is asking where the right to circumcise one's children came from in Old Testament Israel. Did it come from being a biological descendant

68

of Abraham? Or did it come from making a profession of faith just as Abraham did?

If we say that the right to circumcise one's children came from the fact that a person was biologically descended from Abraham, then circumcision would become a physical, ethnic symbol rather than a spiritual one. And if circumcision was merely a physical, ethnic symbol for Abraham's biological descendants, then the link to new covenant Christians breaks down. We no longer have a reason to apply the outward sign of God's covenant to our children, as Abraham did. But, again, we need to ask, Is Kingdon right about these things?

The Obvious Examples of Baptism

One of the strongest objections to the practice of applying baptism to our children comes from the fact that the explicit examples we find in the New Testament are entirely adult baptisms. Although there are at least three clear examples of "household" baptisms,[3] it is nonetheless true that the vast majority are of adult believers. It might seem obvious to some in looking at these examples that baptism ought to be applied only to believers. But is this true? Why do the explicit examples of baptism seem to consist entirely of adults?

The Doctrine of the Church

Another objection to the practice of applying baptism to believers and their children comes from those who see the church as consisting only of believers and baptism as the corresponding rite of initiation into the church. These brothers and sisters are convinced that it is wrong to apply the external sign of inclusion in the new covenant people of God to infants because infants are not included in the new covenant people of God. Only those who have professed faith in Jesus Christ for themselves and thus are members of the new covenant people of God have a right to the external sign of inclusion in this people. Those who make this argument appeal primarily to Jeremiah 31:31–34 (see also Heb. 8:8–12; 10:16–17) for their justification in making these claims.

Here again, if these brothers and sisters are right about the church consisting only of believers, then it is hard to see where the warrant for baptizing our children would come from. But again we must ask, Are they right?

CHAPTER 8

HOW DO WE
RESPOND TO THE
BAPTIST ARGUMENTS?

Before we respond to the Baptist arguments, it bears mentioning for a second time that the baptism debate is a family disagreement. Whatever view of baptism we hold to, we need to remember that we are brothers and sisters in Christ. We are not disagreeing over explicit biblical truths that are essential to believe in order to be saved. The Bible is not explicit in answering many of the questions we have about baptism. If it were, there would be no disagreement. We are, therefore, arguing over the implications of the Bible's teaching about a topic that is not of the essence of salvation. We need to remember that in the midst of our disagreeing and treat each other as brothers and sisters in Christ and fellow members of the body of Christ.

With that in mind, we can now turn our attention to responding to the arguments of our Baptist brothers and sisters. In doing so, we will follow the same outline that we used in the previous chapter. We will look at (1) the discontinuity that is said to exist between the Abrahamic covenant and the new covenant, (2) the discontinuity that is said to exist between circumcision and baptism, (3) the obvious examples of baptism in the New Testament, and (4) the doctrine of the church and whether it has any bearing on the recipients of baptism.

Discontinuity between Abrahamic and New Covenants?

David Kingdon's claims of discontinuity between the Abrahamic and new covenants arise from the fact that he does not see the essentially spiritual nature of the Abrahamic covenant. And because he does not see it, he also does not see the connection between the rightful recipients of circumcision in the Old Testament and baptism in the New. The Abrahamic covenant was not fundamentally a *national* covenant enacted with Abraham and his biological descendants; it was a *spiritual* covenant enacted with Abraham and his spiritual descendants. All those who would believe in Christ—whether in Abraham's day or in ours—are the rightful descendants of Abraham and heirs of the promises of God given to him. Jesus, *the* offspring of Abraham, guarantees this (Gal. 3:16). Furthermore, Paul repeatedly speaks of the Abrahamic covenant in Galatians 3 not in physical or national terms but in spiritual terms. He first refers to Abraham as an example of one who was justified before God in the same way that we are today (v. 6). He then explicitly states that believers are the real sons of Abraham (v. 7). Then he adds that "the gospel" was "preached . . . beforehand to Abraham" (v. 8) and that all "those who are of faith are blessed along with Abraham, the man of faith" (v. 9). In verse 14, Paul describes the "blessing of Abraham" not in physical or national terms but in terms of the "promised Spirit through faith." And in verse 29, we are explicitly told that all who belong to Christ are "Abraham's offspring, heirs according to promise."

When we put these verses together with Romans 4:12—which states clearly that the Abrahamic covenant was made not with Abraham's biological offspring but with those who shared the same faith that Abraham himself had in the Christ who was to come—we see a strong argument in favor of the essentially spiritual nature of the Abrahamic covenant. Even so, Jeremiah 31, and the apparent contrast it draws between the covenants, appears to be standing in our way. What can we say about Jeremiah 31? We will take up that discussion in the next chapter.

Discontinuity between Circumcision and Baptism?

Kingdon's question about where the right to circumcise one's children came from in Old Testament Israel is a good one. Did that right come from simply being a biological descendant of Abraham? Or did it come from making a profession of faith just as Abraham did?

If the question is in regard to the actual practice that developed within Israel after Abraham, it is possible that the administration of circumcision became focused more on nationality than on faith as the generations passed. But if the question is asking what God intended, we can say with great confidence that God never intended circumcision to be applied as a national symbol of ethnicity. God intended it to be an outward sign of an inward and spiritual condition (a circumcision of the heart) that would be applied to those adults who made professions of faith and to their children. For the Jew, the descendant of Abraham, this profession of faith would have at least taken the form of having his children circumcised at eight days old. According to Genesis 17:10, 14, those Jews who withheld circumcision from their children were considered covenant breakers, living in rebellion against God, whereas those who submitted their children to be circumcised were considered covenant keepers.[1] Thus, for a Jew to offer his children up to be circumcised was for him to publicly embrace the Abrahamic covenant and Abraham's God for himself. It was a public profession of faith.

God's intention for circumcision was never ethnic and physical but spiritual. He intended it to be an outward sign administered to uncircumcised adults who made a public profession of faith for themselves in Abraham's God and also to the children of every adult who publicly embraced the covenant for himself. This is the exact same way that we apply baptism today.

Some of our Christian brothers and sisters—perhaps in an effort to minimize the connection between circumcision and baptism—argue that Colossians 2:11–12 does not teach infant baptism. And, of course, these brothers and sisters are right if they are talking about what the passage explicitly states. Paul, to be sure, does not explicitly deal with the issue of the proper recipients of baptism here. But he does imply a clear link between circumcision and baptism by applying both spiritual circumcision and spiritual baptism to the Christian. And since physical circumcision was the outward sign of spiritual circumcision in the Old Testament and physical baptism is the outward sign of spiritual baptism in the New Testament, Paul is also linking physical circumcision and physical baptism. By doing so, he clearly implies that the proper recipients of baptism in the New Testament are to be the same as the proper recipients for circumcision in the Old.

The Obvious Examples of Baptism?

This objection centers on the fact that the majority of obvious instances of Christian baptism in the New Testament are of believers being baptized. In response, we can say first that the presence of these instances is not definitive in and of itself. The mere fact that an event happened in the first century is in no way indicative of whether that event should be repeated in successive centuries. Take Pentecost, for example. The fact that Pentecost happened in the way that it did in the first century says nothing at all about whether every generation of Christians should experience its own Pentecost event. So even if the examples of baptism in the New Testament are of adults, it does not necessarily follow that baptism ought therefore to be administered in the same exact way from that point onward.

Second, it is not a surprise that the vast majority of the examples of baptism in the New Testament are of adult believers. That is what we would expect. The New Testament was written in a context in which the gospel message was being explicitly proclaimed for the first time. The hearers of this message whom we see responding were predominantly adults who had not only never been baptized before but who had also never believed in Jesus. They were first-generation Christians, not second- or third-generation Christians. That necessarily means that the vast majority of baptisms in the New Testament were adult baptisms. The issue comes back to the household baptisms, of which there are at least three. Taken together, the household baptisms and the adult baptisms form a practice that Jews would have been accustomed to since at least Genesis 17.

The Doctrine of the Church?

Does the church consist only of believers in the New Testament? And if it does, what does that say about who the proper recipients of baptism should be? In answering these questions, we will begin by examining the covenant communities of both the Abrahamic covenant and the new covenant in more detail.

With the inauguration of the Abrahamic covenant, we see two different covenant communities take shape. We see the beginning of an external covenant community—a visible community—that is made up of all who embrace the covenant outwardly with their lips and lives but not necessarily inwardly with their hearts. And we also see an internal covenant community—an invisible community—that is made up of all who embrace the covenant inwardly by genuinely believing as Abraham did.

two Israels

Paul speaks of these two communities in Romans 9:6–8 when he tells us that "not all who are descended from Israel belong to Israel" (v. 6). Paul is teaching in this passage that there are really two "Israels" in existence. One consists of Abraham's biological descendants, his "children of the flesh" (v. 8). This is the nation of Israel or what we are calling the external (visible) covenant community. They embraced the covenant at least outwardly with their actions, but they did not all genuinely believe from the heart as Abraham did. The other "Israel" that Paul mentions is a subset of the previous one. It is composed of Abraham's spiritual descendants, "the children of God" or "the children of the promise" (v. 8). This is the faithful "remnant" that existed within the nation of Israel. It is what we are calling the internal (invisible) covenant community. They too embraced the covenant outwardly, but they also embraced it inwardly by sharing the same faith that Abraham had.

The Abrahamic covenant established both of these communities. Both were entitled to receive the outward sign of circumcision, because both acknowledged the place of the covenant in their lives. But only the internal community, which consisted of the spiritual children of Abraham—"the children of the promise" (v. 8)—were truly members of the Abrahamic covenant. The others were members outwardly or in name only.

The same thing is true in regard to the new covenant. When the new covenant is inaugurated, the same two communities are established, or, maybe better, re-established. Thus we see an external (visible) community composed of those who profess faith in Christ with their lips, but not necessarily with their hearts. They embrace the new covenant outwardly. But we also see an internal (invisible) community composed of those who genuinely believe in Christ. They embrace the covenant inwardly with their hearts. Both communities are entitled to receive the outward sign of baptism, because both acknowledge the place of the covenant in their lives. Both profess to believe in Jesus Christ, even though only one community genuinely does. The one that does genuinely believe is the one that is the real new covenant people of God. The others are so outwardly or in name only.

We see evidence for these two new covenant communities in Matthew 13:47–50:

> Again, the kingdom of heaven is like a net that was thrown into the sea and gathered fish of every kind. When it was full, men drew it ashore and sat down and sorted the good into containers but threw away the bad. So it will be at the end of the age. The angels will come out and separate the evil from the righteous and throw them into the fiery furnace. In that place there will be weeping and gnashing of teeth.

In these verses, Jesus portrays the kingdom of heaven as a net that is thrown into the sea. Just as the net is in the sea but is also distinct from the sea, so the kingdom of heaven is in the world but is also distinct from the world. The significance of this can be seen in the fact that Jesus goes on to say that the kingdom—and not just the world—consists of both "evil" and "righteous" people.[2]

In other words, Jesus seems to be saying that the kingdom of heaven on earth will be made up of both an external covenant community and an internal covenant community. It will contain those who embrace the kingdom of heaven at least outwardly and those who embrace it inwardly with a genuine saving faith. Those who embrace it only outwardly, Jesus says, will be "throw[n] into the fiery furnace" where "there will be weeping and gnashing of teeth" (v. 50). They are unbelievers. And yet, we are told that they will live and serve side by side with believers in the kingdom of God until "the end of the age" (v. 49). Thus, it appears that the New Testament and the Old Testament covenant communities will look very much the same. They will both consist of an external (visible) community that professes to believe but may not in actuality and an internal (invisible) community that genuinely does believe.

When we put these two communities alongside of Matthew 16:18–19, we see that the church is not made up of believers only but of believers and unbelievers together. In Matthew 16, Jesus virtually identifies the church with the kingdom of heaven by promising first to build the "church" and then to give His disciples the "keys of the kingdom of heaven" with which to govern it. In saying this, Jesus is indicating that the church is to be the visible expression of the kingdom of heaven on earth. And since, as we have already seen in Matthew 13:47–50, the kingdom will consist of both believers and unbelievers, we know that Jesus is telling us that the church, just like the Old Testament covenant community, will not be made up of believers only but of believers and unbelievers.

If it is true that the new covenant, in substantial continuity with the covenants of the Old Testament, consists of believers who truly have faith and unbelievers who merely profess it, then it makes no sense to limit the application of the external sign of initiation into this people to believers only. In continuity with the covenants of the Old Testament, it makes sense that in the new covenant, the external sign of initiation into the covenant community will be applied to those who profess faith and to their children as well. But before we can definitively arrive at this conclusion, we need to examine Jeremiah 31 in more detail. This passage occupies a central place in the arguments of believers-only advocates. So we will devote the following chapter to looking more closely at what it has to say.

CHAPTER 9

BUT WHAT ABOUT JEREMIAH 31?

As we have seen, Jeremiah 31 holds a central place in most arguments for believers-only baptism. But it is not clear that our Baptist brothers and sisters have understood this passage accurately. In fact, I would suggest that if we dig a little below the surface of each of its verses, we will see that Jeremiah 31 does not actually teach what our Baptist brothers and sisters think it does, that is, it does not teach substantial discontinuity between the new covenant and the Abrahamic covenant. Instead, it confirms that these two covenants are essentially the same. ?

Clear Continuity

We see the essential continuity between the Abrahamic and new covenants in Jeremiah 31:33–34, for instance, when Jeremiah describes the new covenant and how it will be different from all the covenants that preceded it. In laying out these differences, he cites the phrase "I will be their God, and they shall be my people" (v. 33) as being one of the characteristics of the new covenant. This phrase, however, was explicitly included in the promises that God made to Abraham in Genesis 17:7: "And I will establish my covenant between me and you and your off-spring after you throughout their generations for an everlasting covenant, to be God to you and to your offspring after you." Thus, according to Jeremiah 31, the very same promise that was a part of the Abrahamic covenant will remain a part of the new covenant, which quite obviously demonstrates that there is continuity between them.

But we can also see continuity in the fact that the phrase "I will be their God, and they shall be my people" occurs quite extensively in the Old Testament to refer to the *external covenant community*. In Exodus 6:7, for instance, God makes this promise to the physical nation of Israel: "I will take you to be my people, and I will be your God, and you shall know that I am the LORD your God, who has brought you out from under the burdens of the Egyptians."[1] This promise is not reserved for the inward covenant community, those who genuinely believe. It is given to the physical nation of Israel, the biological sons of Abraham. Why would we think that the same promise would now in the new covenant apply only to genuine believers? Plain and simple, we should not. The phrase "I will be your God, and you shall be my people," is not reserved only for believers in the Old Testament. It is given to the external covenant community as a whole, which, beginning at least with Abraham, also included infant children. This, in and of itself, ought to be sufficient to overturn the thesis that Jeremiah 31 teaches substantial discontinuity between the Abrahamic and the new covenants.

But essential continuity can also be seen in Jeremiah 31 in the clear references to divine initiative in the new covenant. Repeatedly, we are told that the new covenant will be defined by a dependence on the same kind of divine sovereignty that defined the older covenants. In the Abrahamic covenant, we are told <u>seven times that God</u> will establish the covenant and that He Himself will bring all of its promises to pass (Gen. 17:2, 5, 6, 7, 8). And, significantly, in the new covenant, we are also told <u>seven times that God will sovereignly establish the covenant and bring its promises to pass</u> (Jer. 31:31, 33, 34). Here, too, the new covenant does not look like a substantially different covenant but one that is very much in keeping with the covenants that had come before.

Dealing with the Apparent Differences

What, then, do we do with the three phrases (in Jer. 31:33–34) that seem to suggest the new covenant will <u>be different</u> from all previous covenants? Those phrases indicate that (1) all the members of the new covenant will have the law written on their hearts (v. 33), (2) they will all be God's people (v. 33), and (3) they will all know the Lord and be forgiven of their sins (v. 34).

We need to begin to answer this question by reminding ourselves that the true members—that is, the members of the internal (invisible) communities of both the Abrahamic covenant and the new covenant are those who genuinely believe as Abraham did and are thus "in Christ," who is *the* offspring of Abraham. We should not be surprised, therefore, that in both covenants we find language used that would apply only to genuine believers. We have already pointed out the example of the phrase "I will be your God, and you shall be my people" in the Old Testament. This phrase, which is given to the external covenant community, refers to them in terms that are particularly reserved for the internal covenant community. Only those who genuinely believe as Abraham did have a right to the promise "I will be your God, and you will be my people." But the promise is given both to believers and to unbelievers in Israel. The same kind of thing holds true in Jeremiah 31 as well. It is speaking of the external covenant community in terms reserved particularly for the internal community.

But, in understanding Jeremiah 31, it is also important to keep in mind the immediate context of the passage. The context is not comparing and contrasting the Abrahamic covenant with the new covenant. The context is dealing specifically with the *Mosaic covenant* and comparing and contrasting it to the new covenant. The point Jeremiah is making is that the new covenant will be different from ("not like"; v. 32) the Mosaic covenant in three main ways: (1) the law will be written on the hearts of the people, (2) all will know the Lord, from the least to the greatest, and (3) God will remember their sins no more. The context is significant for understanding how the new covenant is different in each of these ways. It helps us see that the new covenant is only different in its *form* but not in its *substance*.

We see this first in the promise that God will write the law upon the hearts of the people in the new covenant (v. 33). The law that was written on tablets of stone in the Mosaic covenant will now be written on the hearts of the people. It is not that the law will no longer apply or that it will be replaced by a new law. The law that was a part of the Mosaic covenant will still be a part of the new covenant. The only difference is in the form that law will take.

Second, we see this difference in form in the promise that all in the new covenant will know the Lord (v. 34). Here again, the context shows us that this verse is not suggesting that believers alone will be a part of the new covenant. It shows us that the new covenant will be different from the Mosaic covenant in both its *clarity* and its *universality*. In regard to its clarity, the passage teaches that the new covenant will be one in which God will speak to His people clearly and not under a "veil" as He did under the Mosaic covenant (see 2 Cor. 3:12–16). The gospel, which was definitely integral to the Mosaic covenant, was, nevertheless, obscured by shadows and veiled in darkness. In the new covenant, however, God has turned on the lights, so to speak. He has made the gospel message that was held out to us in the Mosaic covenant clearer and fuller. He has not given us a different gospel or a better gospel in the new covenant than He gave in the Mosaic covenant. He has given us the same gospel, but He has given it to us more clearly and more fully. The veil has been removed. The substance of the covenant has not changed, but the form has.

In regard to its universality, the new covenant is said to be one in which "all" will know the Lord, "from the least . . . to the greatest" (Jer. 31:34). This too is not an indication that every member of the new covenant will be a genuine believer. It is instead a statement that a change in form is coming. Whereas in the Mosaic covenant the knowledge of God and of His will was confined only to the privileged few—the prophets and the priests—in the new covenant, all, *from the least to the greatest,* will have the same access and opportunity to know God and His will. That is why Jeremiah can say that teachers will no longer be necessary in the new covenant. All will have access to what only the privileged few had access to before. In the new covenant, teachers will have more in common with guides than with prophets or priests. They will take others by the hand and lead them to the Lord so that they might be taught by Him (see Isa. 2:2–3). They will help others understand God's revealed will for themselves, but they will no longer be responsible for revealing God's will to them. All will have access to it for themselves. Thus, we see that Jeremiah 31 is not limiting the membership of the new covenant to believers. It is expanding on the promises and privileges given in the Old Testament to Abraham and to Moses.

Third, we see the new covenant's formal difference in the final promise given in Jeremiah 31, namely, that God will remember sins no more (v. 34). Here again, the context helps us uncover what is actually being said. The point is not that the new covenant will be for believers only. The point is that the new covenant will be far superior to the Mosaic covenant. In the Mosaic covenant, God commanded the people to bring continual sacrifices. Over and over again, the people had to come with their sacrifices for their sins. That was because, in the Mosaic covenant, God was still remembering sins. As the author of Hebrews tells us, the blood of bulls and goats cannot take away sins (Heb. 10:4). It was never intended to. It was intended simply to be a stopgap measure until the once-for-all-time sacrifice of Jesus was here. With Jesus' sacrifice, all other sacrifices are unnecessary and obsolete. With Jesus' sacrifice, God no longer remembers sins. He punishes them once and for all in and through the cross of Christ and "forgets" them forever.[2] Once again, the context helps us see that the difference between the Mosaic covenant and the new covenant is not one of substance. It is one of form. The substance remains the same between the two. But the form this substance takes in the new covenant is *far better* than it was in previous covenants.

Rather than teaching that the new covenant is made up entirely of believers, Jeremiah 31 actually teaches that the new covenant is in substantial continuity with all the covenants that preceded it. To be sure, it is not identical to the Mosaic covenant or the Abrahamic covenant. It is different. But this difference is simply one of form. The context of Jeremiah 31 helps us see this. The spiritual nature of the Abrahamic covenant also helps us to see this. Romans 4:11–12 and Galatians 3:16 help put Jeremiah 31 in a different light. We should look not for substantial discontinuity between the two covenants but for only a discontinuity in the form they take.

Conclusion

We can therefore conclude, in contradistinction from our Baptist brothers and sisters, that the difference between the new covenant and all other Old Testament covenants is not that the former will be made only with genuine believers while the latter were made with both believers and unbelievers. The new covenant will be different in form, but the substance will remain the same. That is because "all of the promises of God find their Yes in" Christ Jesus (2 Cor. 1:20). He is the continuity between all of the divine covenants. The form of these covenants, however, is clearly different, as Jeremiah 31 makes plain. The new covenant is superior to every other covenant (Heb. 8:6–7). It is superior because the long-awaited "offspring" of Abraham has finally arrived (Gal. 3:16). All the Old Testament prophecies, types, and foreshadowings have now finally come to fulfillment in the person and work of Christ. The form of the new covenant is, therefore, obviously different—enough so that there is no reason whatsoever to return to the previous covenants; they are now "obsolete" (Heb. 8:13). But the new covenant is essentially the same as the Abrahamic covenant because it was made with Christ, and all who are in Christ are children of Abraham and members of the covenant God enacted with him.

Because there is essential continuity between the Abrahamic covenant and the new covenant, we would also expect to find essential continuity between the outward signs of the two covenants and the ways that they are to be administered. Barring specific instructions to the contrary in the New Testament, this means that baptism ought to be applied in the same way that circumcision was under the Abrahamic covenant. And this means that our children have every right to receive the outward sign of inclusion in God's covenant community.

Sp. birth ?
John 3

CHAPTER 10

WHAT OBJECTIONS DO WE HAVE TO BAPTIZING BELIEVERS ONLY?

O ur brothers and sisters who believe baptism ought to be applied only to believers have a few objections that they must deal with as well, objections that not only seem to call their views into question but that seem to support the position of covenant baptism argued for in this book.

An Incredible Silence

The first objection that our brothers and sisters must deal with is based on an argument from silence, but it is still challenging nonetheless. When we look at the New Testament, we do not see any evidence of any kind of controversy about the recipients of baptism. We would expect to see some kind of controversy if our brothers and sisters are right that baptism should be applied only to adult believers, because what they are suggesting is a *complete reversal* of a practice that God had instituted beginning with Abraham in Genesis 17. If at 8:59 a.m. on the morning of Pentecost, the children of all those who were assembled in Jerusalem were considered members of the covenant community (and as such entitled to all the privileges of that membership), and then at 9:01 a.m. they were suddenly cut off from the covenant community (and as such lost all of the very privileges that they had just minutes before) until and unless they professed faith for themselves, we would expect to see some kind of negative reaction. But we do not see anything of the kind. We see plenty of negative reaction in the New Testament when it was decided that circumcision was no longer required. The Apostles dealt with that issue at great length. But we see no negative reaction, no expression of surprise or concern, and absolutely no questions raised in the New Testament at all about children being removed from the covenant community. Are we to believe that no one objected to this monumental reversal in practice as we transition from the Old to the New Testament? That is hard to believe.

A Complete Contradiction

Advocates of believers-only baptism want us to believe not only that this monumental shift occurred without any controversy or hint of concern but also that it occurred even though it contradicts the overarching principle that we see at work when we move from the Old Testament to the New. As we move from the Old Testament to the New, we do not see a principle of contraction or of narrowing but a principle of expansion.[1] In the Old Testament, God's covenant was limited to the nation of Israel. But in the New Testament, this covenant is expanded to include those from "every tribe and language and people and nation" (Rev. 5:9).[2] Most people understand this. In fact, they understand it so well that we have to work hard to get them to see that the God of the Old Testament really is the same as the God of the New Testament. They see the expansion clearly, and it leads them to conclude that the God of the Old Testament is a God of wrath but that the God of the New Testament is a God of grace. Obviously, this is a misunderstanding, but it is a misunderstanding that is grounded on the truth that there is a clear principle of expansion at work when we move from Old Testament to New.

Let me offer another example. In the Old Testament, we see glimpses of Christ prefigured in types, shadows, and ceremonies and predicted in prophecies. But in the New Testament, our view is expanded, and we see Christ Himself—the great antitype and the grand fulfillment of all the prophecies. As Hebrews 1:1–2 says, God spoke in the past "at many times and in many ways, . . . but in these last days he has spoken to us by his Son, whom he appointed the heir of all things, through whom also he created the world." This is the principle of expansion.

The problem with the believers-only position on baptism is that it runs counter to this principle. It eliminates children from God's covenant community. For thousands of years, they were included, and now, as we move into the New Testament, are we to believe that a principle of contraction is at work in this one area? Are we to believe that God's covenant community has now gotten more restrictive, more narrow, when everything else is expanding?

What about the Membership of Past Covenants?

Some have suggested that there is Old Testament precedent for expanding and contracting the membership of the covenant community. Most notably, these brothers and sisters point to the example of Noah. In the Noahic covenant, we are told that God establishes a covenant between Himself and "every living creature" (Gen. 9:10, 12, 15), between Himself and "the earth" (v. 13), and between Himself and "all flesh that is on the earth" (v. 17). Here the membership of the covenant community seems to expand to include "every living creature" and "all flesh," but then the membership seems to contract again under the Abrahamic covenant, which includes only Abraham and his descendants. If God has thus contracted the membership of His covenants in the past, we should not be surprised if He does it again under the new covenant. If we follow this way of thinking, the Noahic covenant would provide the precedent for the exclusion of children from membership in the new covenant people of God.

Two important comments need to be made in reference to this suggestion. First, the same general context that says that God will establish a covenant between Himself and "the earth" and between Himself and "all flesh that is on the earth" also says that God will establish His covenant between Himself and Noah alone. We see this in Genesis 6:18, for instance, where we read that God tells Noah, "I will establish my covenant with you [singular]." We need to be careful, therefore, about speaking of the extent of the membership of the Noahic covenant until we can figure out how to put these two seemingly contradictory statements together. How can it be that God's covenant is between Himself and "all flesh" on the one hand and also between Himself and Noah alone on the other? This leads us to our second comment.

The context of the account of the flood favors the conclusion that God's covenant with Noah is best understood as made *principally* with Noah and only *secondarily* (and federally) with every living creature. In other words, it appears that the reason why God's covenant has any bearing on "all flesh" is because God has established it in the first place with Noah. We need to remember that it is Noah—and Noah alone—who finds "grace" in God's sight (Gen. 6:8). And we need to remember that it is because of Noah's standing before God as "righteous" that his "household" and "all flesh" are saved with him in the ark (Gen. 6:18–19; 7:1).

Moreover, given the need to "re-create" the earth after the universal destruction of the world by the flood, it should be no surprise that we see striking parallels between God's covenant with Noah and the creation story.[3] But we need to remember that things have now changed with Noah. After God's original work of creation, sin has entered the world. And this means that we ought to expect God's "re-creating" work after the flood to be set in the context of redemption. Thus, we ought to expect God's covenant with Noah to carry implications not only for Noah and his descendants but for all creation as well. This is precisely what O. Palmer Robertson says in regard to the Noahic covenant: "God does not relate to his creation through Noah apart from his on-going program of redemption. . . . The covenant with Noah binds together God's purposes in creation with his purposes in redemption. Noah, his seed, and all creation benefit from this gracious relationship [between God and Noah]."[4] It is because Noah, as an individual, finds "grace" in the sight of God that the implications and blessings of the covenant extend to Noah, to his family, and even to every living creature.

This means that it is best to conclude that there is no real change in covenant membership as we move from Noah to Abraham. Just as Abraham finds favor in the sight of the Lord and all his "offspring" receive the benefits of inclusion in God's covenant community, so the same can be said of Noah (see Gen. 9:9). And if there is no real change in the membership of the covenant community, there is no precedent from which to argue a change in the membership of the covenant community of the New Testament.

The Consistency of the Covenant Baptism Position

Applying baptism both to adult believers and to their children is in keeping not only with the principle of household inclusion that we see in the Noahic and Abrahamic covenants but also with the great principle of expansion that we see as we move from the Old to the New Testament. In the Old Testament, the outward sign of God's covenant was applied only to males. But in the New Testament, the practice expanded to include females as well. Now men and women, boys and girls, receive the outward sign of God's covenant people. There is no contraction, only expansion. Our Baptist brothers and sisters, however, have some explaining to do. Their view of baptism runs counter both to the Old Testament principle of household inclusion and to the New Testament principle of expansion.

A Pastoral Problem

Those who adhere to believers-only baptism also have a pastoral difficulty to overcome. They have no basis upon which to teach their children to pray the Lord's Prayer. How can a child who has not yet professed faith in Christ and, as such, is not a member of God's covenant community, pray the words "*Our Father* in heaven" (Matt. 6:9)? On what basis can they call God "their" Father? They cannot—not until they have professed faith as an "adult" and entered into the covenant community for themselves.

Interestingly—and thankfully—most (perhaps all) of my believers-only brothers and sisters are inconsistent at this point and "borrow" from the covenant view of baptism in the raising of their children. They treat their children as if they are already members of the covenant community (even though their theology says that they are not), and, as such, they disciple them and teach them to pray "Our Father" even from the youngest of ages.

Believers-only baptism also fails to provide for that deep-seated longing within each one of us to have our household set apart to the Lord and marked off as different from all others. Let me explain with an example.

In the congregation where I formerly served, we received a young woman into membership who came from an unchurched background and who married a non-Christian man and had a daughter. Within the first year and a half of her marriage, the Lord changed her heart through a series of providences and wondrously brought her to faith in Jesus Christ. Afterward, she made a public profession of her faith before the congregation and was baptized. But before she stood in front of the congregation to do all this, she came to me privately and said that she really wanted to do something to show that her household was now "different" and that her daughter would now be raised differently than she otherwise would have been. She wanted to stand with Joshua and declare that as far as she was concerned, and as far as her household was concerned, they would be worshiping and serving the Lord (see Josh. 24:15). My response was that baptism is God's way of doing this. It is God's way of marking off the believer's household as "different" or holy, set apart unto the Lord (see 1 Cor. 7:14). There is something in us that longs for that. But apart from a covenantal understanding of baptism, we do not have any basis to provide for it in our theology or our practice.

God has always worked primarily in and through families,

ever since the very beginning with Adam and Eve. We see this emphasized again and again in the Bible. We see it in the narrative of the flood, for example, where Noah's family is saved together with him in the ark. It is because "Noah found favor in the eyes of the LORD" (Gen. 6:8) that the Lord establishes His covenant with Noah (v. 18). And it is because the Lord establishes His covenant with Noah that Noah and his wife and his sons and his sons' wives are all saved (v. 18). But we also see the family emphasized in the life of Abraham, where God's covenant is established with Abraham, and, as a result, with his family, and thus all who are connected with him receive the outward sign of the covenant.

It would be strange if, with the coming of Christ, this family emphasis and approach changed or became less significant. Children under the new covenant are just as much a part of the covenant community as they were under the Abrahamic covenant. They are entitled to the same privileges and blessings and are subject to the same responsibilities that children were then. Jesus ensures this. He is the connection between the Abrahamic covenant and the new covenant. And it is for this reason that we who profess faith in Jesus apply the outward sign of the covenant to our biological descendants just as Abraham and his descendants did in the Old Testament.

CHAPTER 11

WHAT CAN WE TAKE AWAY FROM ALL THIS?

Thus far in our study, we have attempted to address many of the common issues about which Christians have typically disagreed when it comes to baptism. And having done so, we face one final question that needs to be answered before we can bring our study to a close: What can we take away from these things? While it is true that many of the responses we might give will depend on who we are and where we find ourselves, it is also true that there are, nevertheless, a few general things that can be said.

We began our study by showing in chapter 2 that baptism cannot be taken always and only to mean immersion. Although immersion is clearly one valid mode of administering baptism, it is not the only valid mode presented in Scripture. Sprinkling or pouring must also be considered valid as well. The example of the "baptism" of the Holy Spirit at Pentecost in Acts 2 would seem to be enough to demonstrate this conclusively. Because both immersion and sprinkling are presented as valid modes of administering baptism, it is appropriate for our churches to accept either. The Bible emphasizes not the mode of baptism but its meaning. And since the Bible does not emphasize the mode, neither should we.

We showed in chapter 3 that the Bible seems to favor washing or cleansing as the primary meaning of Christian baptism. This is one reason why John Calvin, following Augustine, referred to baptism as a "visible word" that "painted . . . a picture" about the cross of Christ and the washing away of our sins. It is also why Calvin called baptism a "mirror . . . in which we may contemplate the riches of God's grace, which he lavishes upon us." And it is why Calvin went so far as to say that the meaning of baptism—observed in its actual administration—points us to the cross "more expressly" than even the preached Word does.[1]

Third, we argued in chapters 4, 5, and 6 that baptism is to be applied only once, to those adults who profess faith in Christ and have never before been baptized, as well as to the children of at least one believing parent. That is because Jesus is *the* offspring of Abraham and all who are *in Him* are, therefore, the real children of Abraham, both in the Old Testament and in the New. It is because the Abrahamic covenant is essentially the same as the new covenant. While Abraham and his descendants looked ahead to a coming Christ by faith, New Testament Christians look back to the same Christ (whom we see more clearly than Abraham did) by the same kind of faith. It is because circumcision and baptism are both outward signs of an inward and spiritual reality, namely, a righteousness that is ours by faith. And it is because the examples of household baptisms that we see in the New Testament, along with the attitude of Jesus toward little children, can only be rightly understood from a Jewish perspective that considered children to be members of the covenant community and, as such, entitled to receive the outward sign of inclusion in that community.

From these things, we can take away several important implications and begin to apply them in our lives and ministries. We will explore these implications by looking at four main groups of people who are affected by our view of baptism. We will look at the parents of young children, the children themselves, believing adults who have already been baptized, and unbelieving adults who were baptized as young children.

The Parents of Young Children

The first takeaway from this view regarding the application of baptism to the children of believing parents is that it is a very serious matter for parents to withhold baptism from their children or even to delay it unnecessarily. Exodus 4:24–26 is particularly instructive here:

> At a lodging place on the way [to Egypt] the LORD met him [i.e., either Moses or his son] and sought to put him to death. Then Zipporah took a flint and cut off her son's foreskin and touched Moses' feet with it and said, "Surely you are a bridegroom of blood to me!" So

he let him alone. It was then that she said, "A bride-groom of blood," because of the circumcision.

While this passage is difficult to understand for reasons that we cannot get into here, a few things ought to be clear. In the first place, Moses and his wife, Zipporah, neglected to circumcise at least one of their sons. In light of the context, it is likely that it was Gershom, their firstborn. We also know, in the second place, that God was displeased with Moses and Zipporah for their failure, because He had clearly commanded the Hebrew people to circumcise their children even from eight days old. Failure to do so amounted to breaking cove-nant with God, and the penalty was to be cut off from God's people (Gen. 17:9–14). And we know, in the third place, that although the Lord had been patient with Moses' disobedience for several years before this (note that Moses is said to have more than one son in Ex. 4:20, which means that Gershom had gone uncircumcised for at least a couple of years), the fact that Moses would now be returning to the Hebrew people in Egypt as the representative of the Lord and the deliverer of the people meant that his neglect in circumcising Gershom could no longer be tolerated.

Because of the link between the Abrahamic covenant and the new covenant and between circumcision and baptism, it follows that it is just as wrong today for parents to neglect bap-tizing their children as it was for Moses to neglect circumcising his. That is not to say that death will be the necessary conse-quence for those parents who put off their child's baptism, as it clearly was in the case of Moses (Ex. 4:24). That is a leap that is too great for us to make, given the context of the passage and the special office that Moses held and the special role that he played in redemptive history. But it is not too great a stretch to say that the example of Moses teaches us that it is wrong for parents today to neglect the baptism of their children or to put it off unnecessarily.

But other than the negative example of Moses, what positive reasons can we give to encourage parents today to baptize their children? Why should parents in our churches consider embracing this practice wholeheartedly? I can think of four important positive reasons.

The first is because baptism establishes the family as the primary community for Christian discipleship. This seems to have been God's intention for His people from the earliest of days. From at least the time of the Abrahamic covenant, children of professing believers were marked out as belonging to the Lord in a special way. They were not evangelized as "non-Christians." They were discipled and instructed to know the Lord and to walk with Him all the days of their lives. Parents were to teach their children "diligently" and to use every opportunity to talk with them about God and His commands and to set before them a godly example (Deut. 6:4–9). And if they did this, if they "train[ed] up" each child "in the way he should go," they had every reason to believe that "when he is old he will not depart from it" (Prov. 22:6).

Just as circumcision in the Old Testament marked out the households of God's people as belonging to the Lord, so baptism does in the New Testament. It establishes the household as the most basic community of Christian discipleship. Every household with at least one believing parent is a household in which the principle of new life exists. Children who grow up in these households have a unique opportunity. They get the privilege of seeing and experiencing the reality of their parents' faith up close. They are exposed to prayer and to the fruit of the Spirit. And they are discipled and instructed in the way they should go and held accountable to it as they grow and develop. Surely, this is at least part of what Paul means in 1 Corinthians 7:14 when he says that the children of one believing parent are "holy."

The second positive reason is that baptism establishes God's "household" (see 1 Tim. 3:15)—which comprises many individual households—as a corporate community of Christian discipleship. Baptism is the rite of initiation into this "household" (the external covenant community). All who enter God's household in this way receive the privilege of experiencing the same teaching, modeling, and accountability that they would in their individual homes but on a much larger scale. In the church where I formerly served, every member of the congregation promised to do everything he or she could to help disciple every child who was baptized and to reinforce what that child should be experiencing at home. All who are a part of God's household have this responsibility to all who enter it. We are to act as parents to all who enter and to disciple them and direct them in the way in which they should go. Baptism establishes this relationship.

The third positive reason is that baptism, as we have presented it here, visibly proclaims the distinctives of Reformed theology's doctrine of salvation. B.B. Warfield said as much almost one hundred years ago in a pamphlet titled "Christian Baptism": "Every time we baptize an infant we bear witness that salvation is from God, that we cannot do any good thing to secure it, that we receive it from his hands as a sheer gift of his grace, and that we all enter the Kingdom of heaven therefore as little children, who do not do, but are done for."[2]

Everyone knows that infants cannot do anything for themselves. As Warfield says, they "do not do, but are done for." Thus, when we baptize an infant, we proclaim the sovereignty of God in salvation and the complete inability of man to save himself or to do anything to contribute to his salvation. Believers-only baptism has considerably more difficulty in communicating this message clearly. In fact, believers-only baptism seems to be more consistent with a different message altogether: that our salvation is dependent upon something that we must do or a decision that we must make for ourselves.

For those parents who are consciously Reformed in their thinking, this is certainly an important consideration. I would think that these parents would want the baptism of their children to communicate what they have come to know is true about the doctrines of grace. And the more recently these parents have come to discover the Reformed faith, the more strongly they will probably feel about this. In my experience—both as someone who came to the Reformed faith as an adult and as a pastor in a Reformed context who has witnessed many others doing the same—virtually everyone who has come to the Reformed faith later in life is passionate about it. Many such people have described it as coming out of the darkness and into the light. It certainly was so in my experience. And once that kind of change happens in someone's life, there is no looking back. The fact that infant baptism clearly preaches a message that is in keeping with the views of Reformed parents on salvation ought to be an important reason for such parents to consider baptizing their children before they are able to profess faith for themselves.

The fourth reason why parents should consider baptizing their young children is that baptism conveys a real blessing to parents and children alike. We see this when God commands the outward sign of His covenant people to be applied to infants. He does so clearly in Genesis 17:8, and this applies equally in the New Testament as well. But why would God command His people to apply the outward sign of His covenant to young children? The answer is because there seems to be something special about the biological children of His people.

That "something special" is what we see on display in the New Testament accounts of Jesus' blessing the little children—a privilege the likes of which only the Apostles ever received from Jesus. It seems here that Jesus is operating under a covenantal mind-set. He views these children as special, worthy of His time and attention and of His blessing. We also see this something special in 1 Corinthians 7:14, when Paul calls the children of at least one believing parent "holy." Here, too, Paul seems to be operating under a covenantal mind-set. The children he is speaking about are special, but not in and of themselves; they are special because of their relation to the parent who has believed. And we see this mind-set again in 2 Samuel 12:23, when David derives comfort after the death of his child from the knowledge that he will see the child again when he dies. Again, the point seems to be that there is something special about the children of believers.

To be sure, this does not mean that every single child of believing parents is guaranteed of being in heaven. The example of Abraham is enough to show us this. Abraham had two sons, Ishmael and Isaac. Both received the outward sign of God's covenant. Both spent time in Abraham's household under his influence. But only one of them embraced the covenant for himself. Only one believed. And that means that we cannot say the "something special" is a guarantee that the children of believers will necessarily be in heaven. That is saying too much. But there does seem to be a *general* promise here that the children of believers will themselves be believers who are in a right relationship with God. That seems to be the basis of David's hope in 2 Samuel 12. Proverbs 22:6, furthermore, promises that if believers will "train up a child in the way he should go," then *ordinarily* they can expect that when that child "is old he will not depart from it."

Baptism is the sign of this special privilege. It marks out the children of believers as being recipients of it. Surely, parents of young children would want their kids to receive this kind of special blessing from the Lord. So why would they not also want them to receive the outward sign of it as well?

The Children Themselves

After each of my three children was baptized, my wife and I installed decorative plaques or plates on the walls of their bedrooms containing their names and the dates of their baptisms. I would like to say that this was part of a premeditated plan that my wife and I had to teach our children about their baptisms, but I honestly cannot say that. In each case, the plaques or plates were gifts from more discerning family members. We simply hung them up on the walls of the kids' bedrooms. But an interesting thing has happened over the years. The installed pieces have served as conversation starters as the kids have grown and matured. They have given us occasions to talk with our kids about baptism and what it means for their lives.

But these gifts have done more than that for us. They have also helped lay out the path forward in our kids' lives. Two of the gifts contain not only their names and baptism dates but also a transcript of the three questions that my wife and I answered on behalf of our kids when they were baptized. Those questions are as follows:

1. Do you acknowledge your child's need of the cleansing blood of Jesus Christ, and the renewing grace of the Holy Spirit?

2. Do you claim God's covenant promises in [his] behalf, and do you look in faith to the Lord Jesus Christ for [his] salvation, as you do for your own?

3. Do you now unreservedly dedicate your child to God, and promise, in humble reliance upon divine

grace, that you will endeavor to set before [him] a godly example, that you will pray with and for [him], that you will teach [him] the doctrines of our holy religion, and that you will strive, by all the means of God's appointment, to bring [him] up in the nurture and admonition of the Lord?[3]

The plaques have helped point our kids to the path they are to follow. They have helped our kids grow up knowing their parents' commitment to pray for them, to live the Christian life out before them, to teach them, and to strive to raise them "in the nurture and admonition of the Lord." They have helped them grow up knowing the special privileges that they enjoy as covenant children and the corresponding responsibility that goes along with that status. And they have helped them grow up knowing that these things all point toward their embracing the covenant for themselves and toward their looking in faith to the Lord Jesus Christ for their own salvation.

That is one of the things baptism does for children: it lays out the path forward. It lets them know what is expected of them. It is like a family business in which parents involve their children from the earliest years of their lives and expect them to take over when the time is right. The pathway is clear. Everyone knows what to expect.

The gifts that my wife and I received when our kids were young have helped us point to the path forward. But actual baptisms that take place at church over the years can help with this as well, as they provide occasions to engage in discussion about the topic and to connect the dots for our children.

Believing Adults

Westminster Larger Catechism 167 states that every believing adult has a lifelong responsibility to be constantly "improving" his baptism. This somewhat novel idea means that our baptism is not simply to be consigned to the past. It is to have an ongoing impact in our lives until the day we die. It is to function as an ongoing means of grace to strengthen us in our faith, to help us resist sin in our lives and to cultivate holiness, to help us grow in gratitude toward the Lord, and to increase our love for our Christian brothers and sisters.

The catechism says that our baptism does these things when we meditate specifically on the meaning and significance of baptism. If we borrow John Calvin's language in which he speaks of baptism as a mirror, then improving our baptism can be said to first require looking into the mirror.[4] We cannot improve our appearance, so to speak, if we do not know what we look like. Baptism shows us what we look like. It shows us our sin and what Jesus has done to guarantee our forgiveness. It reminds us that we really have been washed by the blood of Christ and are now clean in the sight of God forevermore. We tend to forget these things. We do not see them as clearly over time as we once did. We need to look into the mirror of baptism and meditate upon its meaning and significance. And we need to do this every day of our lives, but especially at those times when we face temptation or when we see baptism being administered. At those times, especially, we ought to look intently into the mirror of baptism and be humbled by our sins, strengthened by the remembrance that Christ died for our sins and was "raised for our justification" (Rom. 4:25), motivated to put sin to death in our lives, thankful that God bestowed His lavish grace upon us, and encouraged to love our Christian brothers and sisters who have been baptized into the same body by the same Holy Spirit.

Because baptism reminds us of what God has sovereignly accomplished for us in our salvation, as Warfield's quote indicates, meditating on our baptism ought also to lead us to worship. It ought to lead us to sing with Isaac Watts,

> While all our hearts and all our songs join to admire
>   the feast,
> Each of us cry, with thankful tongues, "Lord, why was
>   I a guest?
> Why was I made to hear thy voice, and enter while
>   there's room,
> When thousands make a wretched choice, and rather
>   starve than come?"[5]

But in order for baptism to do these things, we must first look. We must first think about what baptism means and why it is significant that we have been baptized.

It is not necessary to be able to remember our own baptism in order to receive these benefits. It is enough to know that we have been baptized and what that baptism signifies. With that knowledge, we are sufficiently armed to improve our baptism every time we see it being administered and every time we think of it.

Unbelieving Adults

But what about those who are baptized as young children and then never place their faith in the Lord Jesus Christ? What does their baptism do for them? In the first place, their baptism functions as a constant call to place their faith in Jesus to be washed from all their sins. It serves as a permanent gospel tract, if you will, that is always in their possession. They can never rid themselves of it. And it constantly calls out to them to embrace the faith of their parents. It constantly reminds them of the lavish grace of the Lord Jesus, which really is greater than all their sins (Rom. 5:20). It constantly beckons them to come and be washed.

But, in the second place, their baptism also serves as a warning of how serious it is for them to persist in their rejection of Christ. As those who have received the outward sign of baptism and have been raised as covenant children, they have had an opportunity to grow up experiencing greater light and greater privilege. And, as Jesus says in Matthew 11:20–24, greater privilege always brings with it a greater responsibility. It will, therefore, be "more tolerable on the day of judgment" (v. 24) for the unbaptized person who rejects Christ, having never experienced the privilege of growing up as a covenant child, than for the one who has been baptized and has enjoyed the blessings of being taught about Christ from the earliest of ages but who rejects these blessings and refuses to believe in Christ.

In the end, however, those adults who have been baptized as young children and never come to faith in Christ are in much the same position as was the Prodigal Son in Luke 15. They have both experienced something of the love of the father and grasped something of his character. And they have both seen the father up close and personal. In the case of the parable, it was the Prodigal Son's experience of the father that called him to return home when the time was right—the text says, "when he came to himself" (v. 17). In the case of adults who have been baptized and never believed, it is this same experience of the Father that is calling them to come home. It beckons to them through all the "reckless living" and all the "squander[ing of] property" (v. 13). It holds out hope that they really will be received by the Father if they will only return to Him—and not simply received by the Father but lavishly welcomed by Him in joyous celebration. That is the hope that baptism holds out to all who have been privileged to receive it.

NOTES

Introduction

1 Mark A. Noll, *The Scandal of the Evangelical Mind* (Grand Rapids, Mich.: Eerdmans, 1994), 12.

2 N.K. Clifford, "His Dominion: A Vision in Crisis," in *Sciences Religieuses/Studies in Religion* 2 (1973): 323; cited in Noll, *Scandal of the Evangelical Mind*, 12.

Chapter 1

1 Most scholars believe that the Septuagint was written beginning in the third century BC. See, for instance, S.K. Soderlund, "Septuagint," in *The International Standard Bible Encyclopedia*, ed. Geoffrey W. Bromiley (1915; repr., Grand Rapids, Mich.: Eerdmans, 1988), 4:400.

2 The Septuagint reading is *baptizō*, which is the most common word for baptism in the New Testament, occurring something like seventy-five times. The ESV translates it as "dipped."

3 The ESV actually reads "various washings," but the Greek is *diaphorois baptismois*, which is literally translated "various baptisms."

4 The eleven ritual "baptisms" in the Old Testament are as follows: (1) the investiture of the priesthood in Exodus 29:4–6; 40:12; Leviticus 8:6; (2) the purification before entering the tabernacle in Exodus 30:18–21; (3) the purification of the Day of Atonement in Leviticus 16:4, 24, 26, 28; (4) the purification of the red heifer sacrifice in Numbers 19:7–8; (5) the purification of the priesthood before the offerings in Leviticus 22:1–7; (6) the purification after touching an unclean object in Numbers 19:11–22; 31:19–24; (7) the purification for leprosy in Leviticus 14; (8) the purification for eating meat with blood in it in Leviticus 17:14–16; (9) the purification from unclean discharges

in Leviticus 15:1–13; (10) the purification from discharges related to reproduction in Leviticus 15:16–33; and (11) the purification from contact with the dead in Leviticus 11:25, 28, 32.

5   See also Genesis 17:11, where circumcision is also called a "sign."

Chapter 2

1   This does not mean that immersion is an invalid mode of baptism. It only means that the word *baptism* itself cannot be taken to refer to the specific mode of immersion.

Chapter 3

1   See John Murray, *Christian Baptism* (Phillipsburg, N.J.: P&R, 1980), 3–5.

2   Murray, *Christian Baptism*, 3.

3   It is primarily because the New Testament is agnostic on the question of the mode of baptism that we can say that immersion is not necessary in order to portray union with Christ. If it were necessary, the Bible would surely have explicitly stipulated it as the only acceptable mode.

Chapter 4

1   John Calvin, *Institutes of the Christian Religion*, ed. John T. McNeill, trans. Ford Lewis Battles (Philadelphia: Westminster John Knox, 1960), 4.15.18.

2   Calvin, *Institutes*, 4.15.18.

Chapter 5

1   There are approximately twelve instances of Christian baptism in the New Testament. They can be found in Acts 2:41; 8:12, 13, 38; 9:18; 10:48; 16:15, 33; 18:8; 19:5; 1 Corinthians 1:14, 16. In four of these instances, it is unclear whether the people being baptized had previously professed faith: Acts 8:38; 19:5; 1 Corinthians 1:14, 16.

2   Those who deny the continuity of Old and New Testaments will have a hard time seeing the legitimacy of our practice of applying baptism to children. The discipline of biblical theology has helpfully and, I think, conclusively demonstrated that the Bible is in fact one great story centered on one great person, Jesus Christ. There are many excellent resourc-

es to help those who may be agnostic on this issue to think it through on a deeper level. See Richard B. Gaffin, "The Redemptive-Historical View," in *Biblical Hermeneutics: Five Views*, eds. Stanley E. Porter and Beth M. Stovell (Downers Grove, Ill.: IVP Academic, 2012), 89–110; Edmund Clowney, *The Unfolding Mystery: Discovering Christ in the Old Testament* (Phillipsburg, N.J.: P&R, 1988); and, for more hardy souls, the classic by Geerhardus Vos, *Biblical Theology: Old and New Testaments* (1948; repr., Edinburgh, Scotland: Banner of Truth, 1975).

3   See, e.g., David Kingdon, *Children of Abraham: A Reformed Baptist View of Baptism, the Covenant, and Children* (Haywards Heath, England: Carey, 1973), 29–34; Shawn D. Wright, "Baptism and the Logic of Reformed Paedobaptists," in *Believer's Baptism: Sign of the New Covenant in Christ*, eds. Thomas R. Schreiner and Shawn D. Wright (Nashville, Tenn.: B&H Academic, 2006), 228–40; Stephen J. Wellum, "Baptism and the Relationship between the Covenants," in *Believer's Baptism*, 153–60.

4   See also Jeremiah 4:4.

5   In Leviticus 26:41, we are told that an uncircumcised heart produces covenant breaking and rebellion against God, and in 1 Samuel 17:36, we see that to be uncircumcised is to be in defiance against God.

6   In Acts 7:51, we read that to be uncircumcised in heart is to be "stiff-necked" and to be "always resist[ing] the Holy Spirit."

7   See also Ezekiel 44:7, 9, for a similar idea.

8   It is true that Ishmael was not circumcised as an infant at eight days old. According to Genesis 17:25, Ishmael was actually thirteen years old when he was circumcised outwardly. But the point is that he was not circumcised on account of his own faith, because we are expressly told that he was excluded from the covenant, meaning that he was never circumcised on the inside (see Rom. 9:7; Gal. 4:24–31). He received outward circumcision not because of his own faith but because of Abraham's faith, the same way that infants at eight days old were to receive circumcision.

Chapter 6

1   At least three of the twelve instances of Christian baptism recorded in the New Testament are household baptisms, and maybe as many as five.

2   Although it is possible that some in Abraham's household may have believed, we know that some at least did not believe—at least not in a way that could be articulated to Abraham so that he would know to circumcise them based on their faith, because they were only eight days old.

3   Significantly, the word "household" in Genesis 7:1 is, in the Septuagint, the same Greek word that occurs in Acts 16 in the accounts of Lydia's "household" and of the Philippian jailer's "household."

4   Remember also that in the Old Testament, God frequently spoke of the external covenant community in terms that really applied to the internal community. The phrase "I will be your God, and you will be my people" is a good example of that. See the discussion on the doctrine of the church in chapter 8 for more on the external and internal covenant communities.

5   Daniel B. Wallace, *Greek Grammar beyond the Basics: An Exegetical Syntax of the New Testament* (Grand Rapids, Mich.: Zondervan, 1996), 632, favors the ESV's interpretation.

6   F.F. Bruce argues that "it is difficult to say" whether the adverbial phrase goes with the verb or with the participle, because, he insists, it could "be taken grammatically with either" one. But he then concludes by guessing that "it probably goes with both." See Bruce, *The Acts of the Apostles* (Grand Rapids, Mich.: Eerdmans, 1990), 365. Bruce's comments underscore the uncertainty inherent in the text and the fact that every translation is also an interpretation.

Chapter 7

1   See Kingdon, *Children of Abraham*, especially chapter 4.

2   Kingdon, *Children of Abraham*, 42.

3   Household baptisms make up at least 25 percent of the total number of instances of baptism in the New Testament. See note 1 on p. 53.

4   Kingdon calls this argument "the strength of [the Baptistic] position" on baptism. See *Children of Abraham*, 60.

Chapter 8

1   Remember that every Jew, as a descendant of Abraham, would already have been circumcised at eight days old. Only his children remained to receive the rite at eight days old.

2   It is sometimes argued, based on Matthew 13:24–30, 36–43, that Jesus is teaching that the world contains both good and bad people (vv. 24–25, 38) and that this ought to color the way we interpret the parable of the net in verses 47–50. But this is to misunderstand both the parable of the weeds and the parable of the net. Jesus does not say in verse 24, "The kingdom of heaven may be compared to a *field*." He says, "The kingdom of heaven may be compared to a *man who sowed good seed*." This means that when Jesus explains that "the field is the world" in verse 38, He is not defining the kingdom. If He had said that the kingdom is like a field, then He would have been defining the kingdom in terms of the whole world. But when Jesus says in verse 47, "The kingdom of heaven is like a *net*," we know that He is defining what the kingdom itself will be like, because He defines it as a net (smaller realm) within the sea (the larger realm). The kingdom (smaller realm) will be in the world (larger realm) but it will be distinct from it. And the kingdom, Jesus says, not just the world, will consist of both believers and unbelievers.

Chapter 9

1   For other occurrences of this phrase as spoken to the external covenant community, see also Exodus 20:2; 29:45; Leviticus 11:45; 22:33; 25:38; 26:44–45; Numbers 15:41.
2   God does not "forget" our sins in the sense that He somehow removes the data from His memory banks but in the sense that He no longer holds those sins against us and no longer allows our sins to affect the way He thinks of us and deals with us. He does not hold our sins against us. He treats us as though we had never committed any of them.

Chapter 10

1   I am grateful to Donald Macleod for first bringing this idea to my attention in his systematic theology lectures at what is now Edinburgh Theological Seminary.
2   To be sure, God's covenant with Abraham was made with gentile believers in mind, as we have discussed above. But this covenant was made primarily with Israel in the Old Testament. It was not until the New Testament that God's covenant is expanded to include the promised "nations."

3 For example, compare Genesis 6:20 and 8:17 to 1:24–25, 30; Genesis 9:1, 7 to 1:28; and Genesis 9:2 to 1:28.

4 O. Palmer Robertson, *The Christ of the Covenants* (Phillipsburg, N.J.: P&R, 1980), 111.

Chapter 11

1 Calvin, *Institutes*, 4.14.6.

2 B.B. Warfield, "Christian Baptism," in *Selected Shorter Writings*, ed. John E. Meeter (Phillipsburg, N.J.: P&R, 1970), 1:329.

3 *The Book of Church Order of the Presbyterian Church in America*, 6th ed. (Lawrenceville, Ga., 2016), 56-5.

4 Calvin, *Institutes*, 4.14.6.

5 Isaac Watts, "How Sweet and Aweful is the Place" (1707).

SCRIPTURE INDEX

Genesis

1	38
1:24–25	122
1:28	122
1:30	122
2	38
6–7	63
6:8	55, 95, 99
6:18	55, 95, 99
6:18–19	95
6:20	122
7:1	55, 95, 120
8:17	122
9:1	122
9:2	122
9:7	122
9:9	96
9:10	94
9:12	94
9:13	94
9:15	94
9:17	94
12	44
15	44
17	44, 47, 54, 56, 57, 58, 59, 60, 61, 62, 63, 92

17:2	83
17:5	83
17:6	83
17:7	82, 83
17:8	83, 108
17:9–14	104
17:10	32, 74
17:11–13	43
17:14	74
17:25	47, 119

Exodus

3:6	5
4:20	104
4:24	105
4:24–26	103–4
6:7	82
20:2	121
29:45	121
29:4–6	117
30:18–21	11, 117
40:12	117

Leviticus

8:6	117
11:25	118

11:28	118
11:32	118
11:45	121
14	17, 117
14:6	16
14:7	19
14:8	19
14:16	16, 17
14:51	16
15:1–13	118
15:16–33	118
16:4	117
16:24	117
16:26	117
16:28	117
17:14–16	117
22:1–7	117
22:33	121
25:38	121
26:41	119
26:44–45	121

Numbers

15:41	121
19:7–8	117
19:11–22	117
19:13	19
19:18–20	19
19:19	19
19:21	19
31:19–24	117

Deuteronomy

6:4–9	105
10:12–13	47
10:16	47
30:6	48

Joshua

24:15	98

1 Samuel

17:36	119

2 Samuel

12	109
12:23	109

2 Kings

5	10
5:1	10
5:10	10
5:14	10

Psalms

51	23
51:2	24
51:7	24
51:10	24

Proverbs

22:6	105, 109

Isaiah

2:2–3	86

Jeremiah

4:4	119
9:25–26	48
31	67, 73, 80, 81–89
31:31	83

31:31–34	66–67, 70
31:32	67, 84
31:33	68, 82, 83, 85
31:33–34	81, 83
31:34	68, 83, 85, 86

Ezekiel

44:7	119
44:9	119

Matthew

3:1	9
3:6	9
3:11	9, 15
6:9	97
11:20–24	114
11:24	114
13:24	121
13:24–25	121
13:24–30	121
13:36–43	121
13:38	121
13:47	121
13:47–50	78, 79, 121
13:49	79
13:50	79
16:18–19	79
19:13	60
19:13–15	60
19:14	61
22:29	5
22:29–32	5
22:32	5
28:18–20	9, 12, 31
28:19	8, 28, 51

Mark

10:13–16	60
10:14	61
10:16	60, 62

Luke

15	114
15:13	115
15:17	115
18:15	60
18:15–17	60
18:16	61
23:39–43	33
23:43	33
24:50–51	62

John

8:56	45

Acts

1:5	15, 24
2	15, 16, 34
2:3	16
2:17	16
2:18	16
2:33	16
2:38	12, 31, 51, 58
2:38–39	58
2:39	58
2:41	118
7:51	119
8	39
8:12	118
8:12–13	36
8:13	37, 118

8:20	37
8:20–23	37
8:21	37
8:36	34
8:38	18, 118
8:9–24	36
9:18	118
10:48	118
15	12
15:1–21	51
16	53, 54, 58
16:11–15	54
16:14	54
16:15	54, 118
16:25–34	56
16:30–32	56
16:31	58
16:33	118
16:34	56, 59
18:8	118
18:24–28	37
18:25	38
18:26	38
19	38
19:1	37
19:1–7	37
19:5	118

Romans

4	45, 46
4:9–11	41
4:11	13, 49
4:11–12	46, 87
4:12	73

4:25	113
5:20	114
6:3	28
6:3–5	26
6:3–6	28
8:8	25
8:9	25
9:6–8	67, 77
9:7	119
9:8	77
12:2	5

1 Corinthians

1	42, 53
1:13	28
1:14	118
1:16	118
6:9–11	24
7:14	98, 106, 108
10:2	16, 28
12:12–26	7
12:13	27, 28
12:21	27

2 Corinthians

1:20	88
3:12–16	85
7:1	24

Galatians

2:3–10	12
3	46
3:6	72
3:7	45, 72
3:8	73

3:9	73
3:14	46
3:16	46, 72, 87, 88
3:29	50, 73
4:24–31	119
5:7–12	12
6:12–16	12

Ephesians

2:8–9	31
5:25–26	24

Colossians

1:27	25
2	51
2:11	48
2:11–12	28, 50, 56, 74

1 Timothy

3:15	7, 106

Titus

3:5	24

Hebrews

1:1–2	93
8:13	88
8:6–7	88
8:8–12	70
9:10	11, 16, 19, 28
10:2	24
10:4	87
10:16–17	70
11:8	44
11:8–10	44
11:9	44
11:10	44
11:15–16	45

1 Peter

3:21	32

1 John

1:7–9	24

Revelation

5:9	93

ABOUT THE AUTHOR

Dr. Guy M. Richard is executive director and assistant professor of systematic theology at Reformed Theological Seminary in Atlanta. He previously served as senior minister of the First Presbyterian Church in Gulfport, Miss., for almost twelve years. He has been teaching for RTS in some capacity since 2010.

Dr. Richard has degrees from Auburn University (B.I.E.), Reformed Theological Seminary (M.Div.), and the University of Edinburgh (Ph.D.). He is author of *What Is Faith?* and *The Supremacy of God in the Theology of Samuel Rutherford*, as well as several articles and chapters. His writing focuses on the theology of the Westminster Confession of Faith and the Reformation and post-Reformation periods.